READ MY LIPS

READ
MY
LIPS

Sexual Subversion
and the End of Gender

RIKI ANNE WILCHINS

Firebrand
Books
Ithaca, New York

Several selections in this book have appeared in earlier versions in the *Village Voice* and *Women on Women 3*.

Copyright © 1997 by Riki Anne Wilchins
All rights reserved.

Book and cover design by Nightwood
Cover and interior photographs by Mariette Pathy Allen
Hair and make-up for cover photograph by Maurice XXX, courtesy of The Beach,
    Greenwich Village (New York City)

Printed in Canada

10 9 8 7 6 5 4 3 2 1

Library of Congress Cataloging-in-Publication Data

Wilchins, Riki Anne, 1952—
    Read my lips : sexual subversion and the end of gender / by Riki Anne Wilchins.
        p.   cm.
    ISBN 1-56341-091-5 (alk. paper). —ISBN 1-56341-090-7 (pbk. : alk. paper)
        1. Wilchins, Riki Anne, 1952-   . 2. Transsexuals—United States—Biography.
    3. Lesbians—United States—Biography.   I. Title.
    HQ77.8.W55A3   1997
    305.9'066—dc21
        [B]   97-30783
                                                                                                      CIP

ACKNOWLEDGMENTS

AS WITH ANY BOOK, THERE ARE MORE PEOPLE TO THANK than room to thank them, but I would like to express my gratitude to: Linda "Colognatollah" Cologna and Caitlin Flowers, for first taking my work seriously and encouraging me to do the same; Joan Nestle, for not throwing me out of her apartment fifteen years ago (as I fully expected) when I practically demanded to be included in the Lesbian Herstory Archives, and, instead, pulling out a tape recorder and spending three wonderful hours with me—your insight and compassion in the years since have been an inspiration; David Valentine, for many insightful and fruitful discussions on our way to demos and vigils, and for shaking, baking, and filleting the chapter on erotics until it began to make sense; Barbara Warren and the New York City Lesbian and Gay Community Center, for years of support and friendship; Judith Butler, whose ideas lit a candle in the center of my life; Lisa Mitchell, for first explaining to me what the hell I was talking about and thus for making this book possible; Kate Bornstein, for being Kate; Jessica Xavier, Denise Norris, Nancy Burkhalter, and Janice Walworth, for dragging me into street activism; Tonye "Hawk" Barreto-Neto and Nancy "Ninja" Nangeroni for chasing around the country from one Menace picketing or demo or murder trial vigil to another—you've always got my back; Dana Priesing, the goddess of all Congressional advocates, for her tireless dedication to making GenderPAC heard on the hill; Alison Laing, for taking lots of heat while I was learning to apply some of the theory to real-life problems and organizing; Nancy Bereano, who turned down the original manuscript for this book—first, for having the idea of how it could be made to work, and second, for having the astonishing lapse of good judgment to publish it; and, of course, all my friends at GenderPAC, the Menace, and S.T.A., without whom I might not be here today.

To Clare Howell

It was my incredible good luck to find in you someone with the same vision and just as desperate for these words. We searched for the same rainbow, but while my eyes looked up, you kept yours on the map and guided us both home.

Without you, this book would never have been written. So this is for you, Clare, and all the others we know still out there, desperate, disheartened, but still anxiously searching the skies, hopeful for any sign of that rainbow.

Contents

Whence come I
and on what wings
that it should take me so long,
  humiliated and exiled,
to accept that I am myself?

Colette, *The Vagabond*

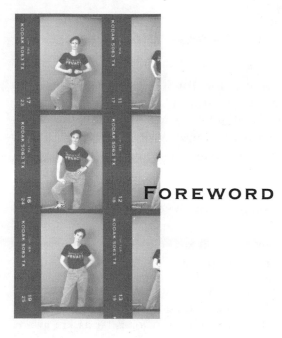

FOREWORD

FIRST OF ALL, SINCE I WEAR SEVERAL HATS (not to mention any number of ill-fitting dresses), I should point out I am not speaking in any official capacity in this book, nor on behalf of any of the organizations of which I am a member.

Second, in any underrepresented community, there is always the danger that the few voices that are lucky enough to be heard end up being cast as representatives. I face the same danger here. This is why I want to emphasize that my opinions are not to be taken as representative of the membership or board of GenderPAC, the coalition of advocacy groups of which I serve as executive director. In fact, few trans-identified folks will agree with everything that is contained in this book. Under the broad label of *transpeople*—which I am too quick to use myself—there is an extraordinarily rich and vibrant diversity. Our own margins, in terms of race, ethnicity, class, and even divergent sub-identities, are still silent and waiting to be heard from. Here's hoping it happens sooner rather than later.

In any case, the idea of being a spokestrans (or spokesherm) has always seemed absurd to me. You lock three transpeople in a sealed room and they'll come out with five opinions among them. We are that opinionated and stubborn; we have to be to survive. So when you read some particularly bizarre sally of mine, rest assured that I am not a community spokestrans, nor do we all sit around discussing postmodern gender theory every night. All the opinions here are my own. Now that I think of it, the ones you like are mine; those you don't were suggested by my editor, or my publisher— probably both.

A WORD ABOUT GENDER ACTIVISM

This book makes no pretense of neutrality with regard to the events that are covered, or what is left out. For instance, the chronology could have started with Anne Ogborn, who, as far as I'm aware, originated the idea of a trans protest movement along the lines of ACT-UP or Queer Nation in 1992 and founded Transgender Nation. Or it could reach back to the first formal radical transorganizations like Street Transvestite Action Revolutionaries (S.T.A.R.), begun in the '70s by Marsha Johnson and Sylvia Rivera after mainstream queer activism had already begun to turn away from its own genderqueers.

But this book is about what I've experienced, a trajectory that took me from a camp in the woods outside the Michigan Womyn's Music Festival to—four years later—handing a letter signed by a dozen members of Congress decrying gender-based violence to an Assistant Attorney General of the U.S. Department of Justice.

My viewpoint is deeply influenced by those events I've either personally witnessed, or in which I've taken a direct part. There are hundreds, perhaps thousands, of people involved in gender activism today, but this book mentions, at best, only a handful of them or their actions.

In addition, some early readers have come away with the conviction that in-your-face picketing-style transactivism originated with the Menace. That's not true, and this is a good place to set the record straight.

WILL YOU BE HAVING ONE S OR TWO WITH YOUR T?

When I was making my interminable way through the Cleveland Clinic's gender program many years ago, some of the Brits working there spelled *transexual* with one *s*. I thought this at least made a single word out of it, since *trans-sexual,* the literal meaning of which I take to be "across sexes," has always seemed absurd.

Since I'd never liked the word to begin with, I stayed with the spelling I liked. This also seemed a way of asserting some small amount of control over a naming process that has always been entirely out of my hands—a kind of quiet mini-rebellion of my own. I think transactivist Dallas Denny captured the spirit of the whole enterprise: "Yeah, we'll change it to one *s* until they all start using it. Then we'll go back to two, or maybe to three." That about sums it up.

FROM C TO SHINING C

While we're on language, I might as well address the dreaded *C* words, both of which you will find herein: cock and cunt. It's not that I get off on being smutty-mouthed (of course I do), but in my experience it's the way people talk.

For those women who find their *C* word distressing, I can only point out that I came of age in a lesbian community in which we reclaimed and employed it with a certain insubordinate and affectionate abandon. I use it in the same spirit here.

ON CONSTITUENCIES: TRANSGENDER V. TRANSEXUAL

Who knows what to call transpeople these days? The dominant discourse in the transcommunity is at best a moving target. *Transgender* began its life as a name for those folks who identified neither as crossdressers nor as transexuals—primarily people who changed their gender but not their genitals. An example of this is a man who goes on estrogen, possibly lives full-time as a woman, but does not have or want sex-change surgery.

The term gradually mutated to include any genderqueers who

didn't actually change their genitals: crossdressers, transgenders, stone butches, hermaphrodites, and drag people. Finally, tossing in the towel on the noun-list approach, people began using it to refer to transexuals as well, which was fine with some transexuals, but made others feel they were being erased. These days, I keep getting asked about the Trans*gender* Menace, and I have to correct the questioner. I know of at least one gay rag (which shall remain unmentioned) that interviewed me and then changed the name of the group in print, a new kind of censorship.

I secretly believe that *transgender* is so popular because people are more comfortable saying it out loud than *transexual*, which—if you hold the word up in the mirror and read it backward—has sex cleverly embedded in it.

Except where noted otherwise, I've used these terms interchangeably, sometimes throwing in *transpeople*, or, to stress the act of self-identification or social categorization, *trans-identified people*.

Although I still use both, during the time since this book was begun this practice has proven unfortunate. *Transgender* began as an umbrella term, one defined by its inclusions rather than its boundaries, coined to embrace anyone who was (in Kate Bornstein's felicitous phrase) "transgressively gendered."

Alas, identity politics is like a computer virus, spreading from the host system to any other with which it comes in contact. Increasingly, the term has hardened to become an identity rather than a descriptor. I recently had a butch tell me she didn't want to co-opt "my voice" and so only identified herself as "small *t* transgender." This is a woman wearing slacks, men's shoes, a man's vest, and so on. In later (and unrelated) incidents, others asked if it didn't make me angry that so-and-so was publicly identifying as transgender because she wasn't "really" a transexual, being "only" a drag person, or an intersexual, or a crossdresser.

The result of all this is that I find myself increasingly invited to erect a hierarchy of legitimacy, complete with walls and boundaries to defend. Not in this lifetime.

I have begun speaking simply of gender as a name for that system that punishes bodies for how they look, who they love, or how they feel—for the size or color or shape of their skin. I do this not to collapse differences, but to emphasize our connections. Dana Priesing, GenderPAC's Washington lobbyist, increasingly tries to employ broad-based, inclusive terms like *gender-different* or *gender-oppressed.*

But at some point such efforts simply extend the linguistic fiction that real identities (however inclusive) actually exist prior to the political systems that create and require them. This is a seduction of language, constantly urging you to name the constituency you represent rather than the oppressions you contest. It is through this Faustian bargain that political legitimacy is purchased.

I only regret that I have succumbed to this very seduction in too many places. For this is not a book about identities, but about a common cultural machinery—one that repudiates, stigmatizes, and marginalizes many kinds of people. It is a book for anyone committed to changing that system.

On Appropriating Experiences and Absent Friends

To the extent that anyone feels neglected, or any readers feel I have misappropriated or misapplied their experience, I apologize in advance, for this was not my intent.

In Closing

This book has been a labor of love, inspired by the many people whose wisdom and courage have helped save my life. I've tried to write the book I needed sixteen years ago. Please feel free to take what you like and leave the rest.

WHY THIS BOOK

THE FIRST TIME I'D SEEN WHITE CUFFS LIKE THESE was in my women's incest group. It happened that two of us were trans-identified. We'd kept fairly quiet out of fear, although, in truth, I was pretty much "out."

Our fears were not misplaced: after a year of unremarkable participation, the casual mention that one of us was "pre-op" blossomed quickly into weeks of acrimonious exchange. We looked on in silence, gripped by a kind of dazed fascination, as people we thought we knew discussed us amimatedly in the third person, as if we weren't there. In a sense, we weren't.

While part of me listened to the argument over whether we were "women enough" to stay, another part quietly wondered how it was that only my identity and body were suddenly "in play." Who had made these rules so others got to vote on me in a way that I was not symmetrically empowered to vote on them? Why were their bodies a priori legitimate while mine was somehow the product of group resolution? And how was it that I knew, even if the vote went in our favor, we would have already been disempowered?

I did not know. I lacked the conceptual tools to understand anything about my situation except that it hurt. I wouldn't have any answers until years later.

It was during this time, in the lull of an inexplicably calm Thanksgiving meeting, that a woman blew like a winter breeze through the crack in our door, folded herself onto the edge of the gunmetal gray chair nearest the exit, and, perching there, began quietly examining the linoleum floor as if it contained the key to the scriptures. By unspoken agreement, we shared in a "go-around" that night so she wouldn't have to raise her hand to speak.

We needn't have bothered. She bolted the room without a backward glance when her turn came, leaving a wraithlike hole where she'd sat. Then it was the rest of us carefully examining the floor, until someone quietly mentioned the white tape on her wrists.

There had been two others after that. One was my friend Hannah, a sculptor. She'd nearly severed her hand in a radial arm saw when she was eighteen. She swears she was lucid and calm at the time; yet she was also so desperate, lonely, and disconnected, she hoped it would kill her, or bring someone running—anyone— who'd finally listen to the pain inside her.

The other was Christine, a guitarist, writer, and sometime working-girl. Trying to escape from her life for one night, she stoned out on a mix of booze and PCP. Then, using the sharp blade of a sword, she severed the fingers of her guitar-picking hand right above the top knuckle, one-two-three-four, and didn't feel a thing until the next morning. The cops had seen this particular tranny in the tank so many times they didn't even try to have her fingers sewn back on.

And then, of course, there's Susan here. Her hands on the steering wheel look strong and capable in the bright Georgia sunlight. I have just come from addressing an indifferent Atlanta Pride parade audience on this hot June afternoon. She is winding her car along the endless freeways, expertly negotiating each turn and on-ramp, hauling me back to the air-conditioned Delta lounge and my plane to New York.

The baking heat must have made me more brain-dead than

usual, because only now do I notice her wrists. Around each, barely above the coffee tan of her hands, are two bands of surgical cotton gauze so immaculate and neatly taped they look for all the world like a matching pair of white shirt cuffs.

There is something peculiarly incestuous about trans-experience. It robs us of our bodies, our intimate moments, our sexuality, our childhood. It robs us of honesty, of open friendship, of the luxury of looking into a mirror without pain staring back at us.

It means hiding from friends and family, from spouses and children, as surely as it means hiding from the police car during an evening stroll, or from that knot of laughing boys down at the corner when we go out for a Coke. In the end, it is as tiring as a constant pain and as barren as the bottom of an empty well at high noon.

So why, with the surge of trans and gender theory flooding from the presses, does so little address or assuage our pain? Why is it mostly irrelevant to translives? Why have all the observations and theories been so utterly useless for transpeople themselves?

The earliest works were usually about people in rehab somewhere. The psychiatrists who wrote them inspected our fetishes, fixations, and gender confusions, producing carefully distanced narratives which were couched in the obscure, analytic language of dysfunction and derangement. We were patients.[1]

Then came the feminist theorists who—while erasing our own voices, and without soiling their pages with the messy complexities of our lived experience—appropriated us as illustrations for their latest telling theories or perceptive insights. We had become examples.

Upon us now is the "transgender studies" anthology, a ticket to an academic grant and a book. These come from earnest anthropologists and sociologists who study us as if we were some isolated and inexplicable distant tribe.[2] Their gaze is firmly fixed on such pressing issues as our native dress, social organization, kinship structures, and relationship with the local gender witch doctors. They employ the objective and nuanced language of ethnography. We have become "natives."

Is there not something deeply immoral in the way these writers fail to help those whose lives they blithely mine for new insights and incantations? Do they never feel a twinge of guilt as their "studies" merely escalate the politicalization of our bodies, choices, and desires, so that, with each new book, while their audience enjoys the illusion of knowing more about us, we find ourselves more disempowered, dislocated, and exploited than before?

Aren't you still a male? Do transpeople reinforce gender stereotypes? Are you a "third sex"? Why do transpeople divide themselves up into men and women—shouldn't you be "gender-free"? Is sex-change surgery voluntary mutilation? Is transgenderism a pathology or mental disorder, and is it learned or genetic?

Academics, shrinks, and feminist theorists have traveled through our lives and problems like tourists on a junket. Picnicking on our identities like flies at a free lunch, they have selected the tastiest tidbits with which to illustrate a theory or push a book. The fact that we are a community under fire, a people at risk, is irrelevant to them. They pursue Science and Theory, and what they produce by mining our lives is neither addressed to us nor recycled within our community. It is not intended to help, but rather to explicate us as Today's Special: trans under glass, or perhaps only gender à la mode.

Our performance of gender is invariably a site of contest, a problem which—if we could but bring enough hi-octane academic brainpower to bear—might be "solved." The academician's own gender performance is never at issue, nor that of the "real" men and women who form the standard to which ours is compared. Through the neat device of "othering" us, *their* identities are quietly, invisibly naturalized. How nice to be normal, to know that the gender-trash is safely locked in the Binary Zoo when they turn off the word processor at night.

No one bothers to investigate the actual conditions of our lives or the lives of those we hold dear. No one asks about the crushing loneliness of so many translives, or about sexual dysfunction. Nor does anyone question why so many of us have to work two minimum-wage jobs and suck dick on the side so we can enjoy the benefits of a surgical procedure theorists and academics are casually debating for free.

No one does an exposé about people like my friend Sarah, who was busted for soliciting. Aware that they had no case and that the judge would let her walk the next morning, the cops tossed her—high heels, make-up, short skirt, boobs and all—into the men's tank, and closed the stationhouse door behind them as they left. She was forced to have sex with forty-two men just to survive the night and, by the time the sun came up, she did walk without having to see a judge. But then, she had already served her sentence.

No one writes about the scores of us who lose our children in custody battles, or the trans-teens who contract HIV by sharing dirty needles because insurance doesn't cover hormones and their parents have thrown them out on the streets. No one researches the special struggles of transpeople of color, or documents the life of my friend Francis, who transitioned in a wheelchair and had bricks thrown through her windows at night.

Nobody inquires why so many transpeople are survivors of incest, child abuse, and outright rape, or what might be done to remedy these crimes.

No one writes about the names we cannot forget, names we still hear in the night—like Christian Paige, a young woman who moved to Chicago to earn money for surgery and ended up brutally beaten, strangled, and then stabbed in the chest and breasts so many times that her family at first thought her body had been intentionally mutilated. We don't hear about Marsha P. Johnson (drowned), Richard Goldman (shot by his father for crossdressing), Harold Draper (multiple stab wounds), Cameron Tanner (beaten to death with baseball bats), Mary S. (fished out of the trunk of her car—beaten, stabbed, and drowned), Chanelle Pickett (strangled), Brandon Teena (raped, beaten, stabbed, and shot), Deborah Forte (strangled and stabbed), Jessy Santiago (beaten, repeatedly stabbed with box cutter, screwdriver, and knife), or her younger sister, Peggy, also transgendered, who was killed just three years earlier.

I carry with me a small slip of paper from Camp Trans, "the

educational event across the road from the Michigan Womyn's Music Festival," as a reminder of what is really at stake in the struggle over translives. Out of thirty of us at Camp Trans, twelve were trans-identified. We were mostly white, mostly middle and working class, from big cities and small towns, many with at least a year or two of college. In other words, except for being trans-identified, there was nothing exceptional about us.

Whenever I see such courage and determination I assume there's a lot of survivorship at work and so, on a hunch, I did a makeshift poll, walking casually from person to person as they munched down cold cereal and hot eggs in the morning mist. After a while, folks started coming up, peering over my shoulder to check the growing tally. Their jaws would tighten, but none looked particularly surprised.

I make no pretense at formal validity, but based on a population of twelve, here are the results:

Incested	5 (40%)
Sexually abused as a child	9 (75%)
Physically abused or beaten (as a child or adult)	12 (100%)
Raped	6 (50%)
Shot	2 (16%)
Stabbed	3 (25%)
Arrested	6 (50%)

In addition, one of us had been burned and one of us had been horsewhipped.

You won't find any of this in the next trans or gender studies book because the real challenges of our lives aren't perceived as relevant to anyone's theory.[3] It is far easier to invest *us* as a topic of study than the depredations of the gender regime which marginalizes and preys upon us. As if one could analyze any ghetto in complete isolation from the conditions and forces that create and maintain it.

Trans-identity is not a natural fact. Rather, it is the political category we are forced to occupy when we do certain things with our bodies. That so many of us try to take our own lives, mutilate ourselves, or just succeed in dying quietly of shame, depression, or loneliness is not an accident. We are supposed to feel isolated and desperate. Outcast. That is the whole point of the system. Our feelings are not causes but effects.

The regime of gender is an intentional, systemic oppression. As such, it cannot be fought through personal action, but only through an organized, systemic response. It is high time we stopped writing our hard-luck stories, spreading open our legs and our yearbooks for those awful before-and-after pictures, and began thinking clearly about how to fight back. It is time we began producing our own theory, our own narrative. No one volume can hope to achieve all this. At best, this is a rough set of beginnings.

I intend to wage a struggle for my life. I intend to fight for my political survival. And until other authors wade down into the deep end of the pool and confront the challenges we face every day, until their gender is seen as just as queer as mine, then they are simply another part of the system I seek to overturn.

So this book is dedicated to those who have shared some of this experience: this having one's body and life captured and held hostage, made to bear witness against one's own deepest meanings, this abduction in broad daylight. It is to trans-identified bodies, incested bodies, aging bodies, fat-identified bodies, intersexed bodies, differently abled bodies—to any and every kind of body which has been stigmatized, marginalized, and made to bear unbearable meanings—that I write.

And it is to the people with the neat white cuffs that I speak. Some wear them on the outside, some on the inside. In the end, only they will judge my success or failure.

1. There is an excellent term in medicine for this kind of practice: *iatrogenic*. Iatrogenic medicine, such as blood-letting by leaches or treatment with arsenic, actually creates disorder and disease, sometimes the very one it is intended to treat. I believe any categorical system of knowledge that creates and maintains people like me as a "pathology" ought to be described as an iatrogenic epistemology and named for what it does: i.e., naturalizing some bodies by creating mine as a kind of disease.

2. My anthro-apologist friend David Valentine has coined the verb *to tribify* (TRÍ-beh-fi) to name this propensity of social scientists to naturalize their own gender and genitals while treating mine as if they were the product of some quaint practice by an "exotic" or foreign tribe.

3. For a wonderful counterexample of engaged and relevant academic inquiry, see Ki Namaste's remarkable "Genderbashing: Sexuality, Gender, and the Regulation of Public Space" in *Environment and Planning D: Society and Space* 14 (1996): 221-240. She mines the critical issue of transviolence, but only to tease out and interconnect wider issues of all gender-based violence. In addition, she does so without stigmatizing her transgender subjects. The focus of her study is the workings of the gender regime itself—the ways violence is used to regulate gender in public space—and not just transpeople as (detached) subjects.

17 Things You DON'T Say to a Transexual

DON'T #1. "I was just talking to A CHANGE the other day and..."

To me, this suggests that you are having strange conversations with your pocket money. No one IS a change. One can ask for change, own change, *ex*change, change tires, change clothes, change sides, change to a minor key, and have a change of life, but one cannot BE a change.

DON'T #2. "You look just as good as I do."

Of course I do. And this is precisely the state of grace to which we all aspire. But more than likely, you do both of us an injustice.

DON'T #3. "Well, I want you to know that I certainly consider you a woman."

It is a never-ending source of wonderment that well-intentioned, and otherwise very well-brought-up people say this to me, with a light of total sincerity shining in their eyes for which any self-respecting cocker spaniel would kill.

Unfortunately, this assurance turns on at least four assumptions which, upon closer inspection, prove to be unfounded: (a) my gender is a subject about which reasonable people might be expected to reasonably differ; (b) my gender is a topic that is currently open for discussion; (c) my gender, and your perception of it, is something about which I suffer rather a great deal of anxiety and about which I am seeking some reassurance; and (d) you, since you are a nontransexual, are in just the providential position of providing me with this reassurance I so desperately seek.

DON'T #4. "I THINK YOU'RE AS MUCH A WOMAN AS ANY OF MY FRIENDS."

What a treat for them. Especially your male friends.

DON'T #5. "I WOULD NEVER HAVE GUESSED YOU WERE A TRANSEXUAL."

This phrase is usually accompanied by a look of the utmost incredulity, followed closely by a searching, penetrating, and largely sotto voce reappraisal of all the things you thought you knew about me (or, perhaps, only all the times we slept together). Unfortunately, this utterance assumes that your credulity, no doubt a topic of endless fascination to you, is of equal interest to me. Since there are tens of thousands of us (maybe in your building alone!), the fact that some of us can "pass" (a nasty concept if ever there was one) as nontransexuals only prophesies that, wedded to the entirely fragile notion that you should be capable of identifying all of us on sight, you are destined for a life of more or less unending private humiliations.

DON'T #6. "CAN YOU HAVE AN ORGASM?"

Yes, but only when I'm asked this question.

DON'T #7. "CAN YOU HAVE AN ORGASM?"

DON'T #8. "CAN YOU HAVE AN ORGASM?"

DON'T #9. "YOU MUST HAVE HAD A LOT OF COURAGE TO FACE SURGERY."

To have the actual surgery, I just had to be able to breathe deeply, count at least partway backward from one hundred, and fall asleep with some semblance of dignity. In all of these tasks I was reliably aided by enough anesthesia to subdue a small water buffalo. It would also have helped had I ten-to-twenty thousand dollars in spare change (see #1 above). Unfortunately, while I was thus drifting majestically off to sleep, I found I also had to be able to watch my friends, most of my lovers, all of my family, and any lesbian who used the term *politically correct* in any context other than a Lily Tomlin joke, fade out of my existence forever. Also, I found that I woke up to endless refrains of DON'Ts #1-8, above. That is the hard part. The surgery I could probably do again before breakfast.

DON'T #10. "I DON'T THINK IT'S ANYONE'S CONCERN WHAT'S BETWEEN YOUR LEGS, UNLESS THEY'RE SLEEPING WITH YOU."

Well, yes. But you, like me, might be surprised at the profound lack of fastidiousness some people display to even this tender area, as my weekly trips to the accoutrement racks at the Pleasure Chest and Eve's Garden confirm. In any case, I'm quite certain that whatever is between your legs, even during those hot, sticky, yucky days of summer, is totally above reproach and perfectly charming, while what's between mine, even on the very best of days, is, well, let's just not talk about it.

DON'T #11. "I THINK TRANSEXUALS ARE JUST MEN IN DRAG."

Of course you do, and you're entitled to your opinion. You can even be justifiably proud to think so. Do not, however, voice this sentiment while surrounded by a room full of men who really *are* in drag (for instance, at the next Fantasy Ball). Also, be certain to note the exception to this rule, which is, of course, female-to-male transexuals, who are really, well, just women in drag. We all know how naturally distasteful it is when men wear dresses or women wear pants. Do not, however, voice this sentiment while surrounded by a room of S/M dykes in full leather and studs.

DON'T #12. "I HEAR YOU'RE A TRANSEXUAL. WHEN DID YOU HAVE SURGERY?"

Yes, and I hear you're a homosexual: when did you first suck cock? Ohhhh—it's not about sex.

DON'T #13. "I THINK OF TRANSEXUALITY AS A KIND OF BIRTH DEFECT."

So do I. I was born into the wrong culture.

DON'T #14. "HOW DID YOU KNOW YOU'RE A WOMAN?"

How did *you* know you were a woman? Ah-hmm: breasts and vagina. Well, I can introduce you to some very handsome, bearded, muscular young men of my acquaintance who began life with the very same equipment, so that's not particularly compelling evidence, is it?... I see, inside YOU just know. Call me sometime, we'll have lunch.

DON'T #15. "IS IT TRUE THAT TRANSEXUALS ARE 'WOMEN TRAPPED IN MEN'S BODIES'?"

Yes, that's right. In my own case, they had to call in both the Fire Department and the EMS and even then it took them hours to cut me out. Luckily I had my Walkman and some wonderful Judy Garland tapes, so it wasn't too awful a wait.

DON'T #16. "YOU LOOK JUST LIKE A REAL WOMAN."

How splendid, especially when you recall I'm composed almost entirely of compressed soy by-products. And you look just like a REAL transexual. Oh, I'm so sorry, I didn't realize that was an insult.

DON'T #17. "ISN'T IT AMAZING, YOU'RE THE ONLY TRANSEXUAL I KNOW."

Yes, and isn't it amazing that when you came out to your mother, you were the only homosexual she knew. Ho-hum. The fact that I am the only transexual you know only emphasizes that: (a) you probably know a few hundred of us but you don't know you know us, and we won't tell you that you do; (b) there are tens of thousands of us, and more all the time; (c) we are secretly plotting to take over the planet Earth, and infiltrating your prevailing non-transexual culture is just the first step; and (d) while we are waiting to take over your planet we are amusing ourselves at your expense by seeing just how much we can fuck with your heads.

What Does It Cost to Tell the Truth?

I WAS TWENTY-SIX WHEN I LEARNED I was very tall. For most of my life I had been considered normal height. But at twenty-six, suddenly, strangers in elevators began leaning toward me conspiratorially and asking, "How tall are you, anyway?" as if we'd been having a conversation on the subject. There were delivery men who inquired, "You play roundball?" and even one man on a motorcycle who slowed alongside me to exclaim, "You must be a volleyball player!"

Although I had never before worried about my height, I began studying myself in mirrors. I began *seeing* myself as tall. In short order, I became self-conscious about the length of my body. I stooped fashionably while walking down the street, tried not to stand up too straight in bars or at parties, and leaned against walls and pillars when speaking so I wouldn't appear to be towering over shorter people.

WELCOME TO GENDERHELL

I learned a lot of other things about my body as well. My voice was unnervingly deep. My hands were too large, my shoulders too broad, my hips too narrow, and my feet much too big. The same size basketball sneakers I'd been wearing for over ten years suddenly looked ridiculous, even to me. People made public jokes about my "boats." I stopped wearing them, even stopped shooting hoops. Although I'd been slender for decades, since I was now "too big," I stopped working out at the gym as well.

I was obsessed with how I looked and was perceived. I became a ferocious shopper, lusting after any clothing that would hide my height and shoulders. I bought winter gloves and dress shoes a size too small. My pinched hands and feet went along with the higher voice I practiced when speaking on the phone.

Over a terrifyingly short period of only one year, my entire perception of my body changed to match the social truths everyone else read there. The mirror, formerly a friend, turned into a deadly enemy. I felt humiliated, ashamed, each time I looked in it, weeping quietly in dressing rooms and loudly at home. I appeared ridiculous to myself because I was seeing what I was told was there: this absurdly tall person with large hands, ungainly feet, wide shoulders, a deep voice, and a masculine manner. Need I go on? What is most remarkable is that I had been about the same size and shape since I was fifteen.

READ ANY GOOD WOMEN LATELY?

What had happened was that I'd started being read by others "as a woman."

That my body became the site of all kinds of social inspection and pronouncements didn't surprise me. But the virulence did. I was accosted from every direction: from the men who hissed at me on street corners; to the man on the train who leaned over and said, "Nice tits," as I boarded; to the construction workers who whistled or yelled, "Faggot!"; to the driver who rolled down his window at a crowded intersection, the very first time I went out in a dress, to shout, "God, you sure are uuug-ly!"

In many ways I imagine that what happened to me is not much different from what happens to many teenagers once their bodies hit puberty and are seized by the cultural machine. In my case, though, I already had a stable body image, and I was an adult, fully aware of what was going on. It shocks me to this day how quickly I learned to make my body over, to embrace the various social truths about it, and to see on it what I was told. I knew what people were thinking when they looked me up and down, stared at my body parts, and inspected my face.

TELL ME HOW I LOOK

"People being introduced to me no longer make eye contact—they make crotch contact," a friend, just starting to be read as a woman, told me.

My body, like hers, heretofore just a place to put food, carry out certain operations of pleasure, and get me from point A to point B, had overnight become an armed camp which I surveyed at my peril. It hurt to be me, and it hurt to see me.

I am reminded of a recent meeting with a transexual female friend of mine. She had begun living full-time as a woman, and eagerly showed me pictures of herself in make-up and various outfits. Again, this is much like any teenager would do. What particularly struck me was that, as she anxiously scanned my face for a reaction, she said, "I have to depend on other people to tell me how I look because I don't know how to see myself yet."

How strange that she was soliciting this information from someone who customarily walks around with a short, butchy haircut, wearing no make-up, dressed in blue jeans, sneakers, and a large black Transexual Menace T-shirt. Which is to say that I do not, at first blush, inspire confidence as the best possible judge of such matters. I could not care less how either of us is read by nontransexuals.

NO ADMISSION TO LIFE WITHOUT A VALID GENDER ID

How does it happen that the human subject makes himself into an object of possible knowledge, through what forms of rationality, through what historical necessities, and at what price? My question is this: How much does it cost the subject to be able to tell the truth about itself?

Michel Foucault, "How Much Does It Cost to Tell the Truth?"[1]

Foucault asked about the necessity of making one's self an object of possible knowledge, to be learned and memorized. For genderqueers, that necessity is survival. The purpose of a gender regime is to regulate these meanings and to punish those who transgress them. In order to survive, to avoid the bashings, the job discrimination, and the street-corner humiliations, my friend will be forced to place herself as a site of *truth* to be mastered. That knowledge will come from others. She must know how others see her so she can know how to see herself; otherwise, she enters society at her peril.

She will gradually learn how she looks and what her body means. She will carry this knowledge around, producing it on demand like pocket ID when she enters a subway car, applies for a job, approaches the police for directions, uses a women's room, or walks alone at night past a knot of men. Summoning up the image in her mind's eye, she will recall the truth of her looks, checking it quickly to determine if anything is "wrong," feeling shame at her shortcomings and pride in her attractive features.

Like me, she may find herself growing further and further from direct sensation, so that in small, gradual steps it becomes successively less important what her body *feels like* than how she *feels about* it. As the source of what her body means becomes more firmly lodged in the perceptions of others, she may experience a curious and distressing sense of dislocation and vulnerability. This ID that she carries—her body—will be continually subjected to being displayed, stamped, and judged.

Since her status and legitimacy as a woman will always be at risk, always be determined by and dependent upon others, she may find that her lack of contact with sensation grows along with a nagging sense of bodily disorientation. She will wake one day to find herself lost within the unfamiliar landscape of her own body, like a nomad in some strange and foreign desert, surrounded by unknown landmarks and inhabited by those whose alien features, and distant ways, she can no longer recognize.

What does it cost to tell the truth?

A DACHSHUND PONDERS WIENER-PEOPLE

Someone out there is undoubtedly saying, "Well, all this is very moving, but there *is* a reality to bodies and you can't get around it. For starters, compared to other women, you are tall." Such a comment highlights my point.

We like to think, in Judith Butler's memorable phrase, that physical features exist somewhere out there "on the far side of language."[2] But if even a feature as fundamental and measurable as my "tallness" can only be derived through your reviewing a population of bodies, perceiving some normative measure, and then carrying out (albeit unconsciously) an operation of comparison, then that tallness looks suspiciously to me like something you read on me instead of some innate feature in me. My measurable height may not be arguable; what it *means* is.

Characteristics of mine that are truly innate, that originate "on the far side of language," ought to be totally apparent to you whether you'd ever seen another human being or not, even if you'd only seen me mounted like the gendertrash insect I am, even if you were a Martian seeing your first humanoid, or a wiener-dog viewing its first vertically challenged primate. Any other readings of my body are culturally relative, contingent upon the context in which you locate me. Hence, if we lived among the Munchkins, you'd argue I was naturally a giantess, while if we lived among the New York Knicks, you'd insist I was somewhat short.

The response to deconstructing the body in this way is frequently to offer up counterexamples, of which skin color is the most common. That line of reasoning goes like this: "Perhaps you're right. Perhaps *some* things about bodies are culturally constructed. But some features are simply there. For instance, what about race? Surely color is just color and not some cultural by-product."

Not so, I say, for while skin color itself may be on the far side of language, nearly everything else we can know about it and all that is culturally resonant is not. Such resonances are often specific to particular subcultures. *Black,* for example, is a peculiarly

American phenomenon. White Americans often see only "African-American" or "black" when they look at someone who appears darker-hued than they are. This perception unconsciously follows the notorious "one drop rule,"[3] a bizarre invention of white America which historically held that "one drop" of African blood made a person black. Yet most black Americans are able to see the complex range and variety of shades in which skin color can come. Since being white has been supremely privileged, and therefore required no further qualification, specific shades of brown or black have held tremendous significance and implications for surviving within a racist system.

EVERYONE'S ANSWER IS THE ONLY ANSWER

Each era in history considers its own embrace of the body's features as "natural" and eternal. But bodies, like all cultural products, go through periods, phases, and even fashions. Consider the breast in the recent American landscape. Only a few decades ago the duckbilled breast, as shaped by the tortured duckbill-shaped bra, was the standard of beauty. Shortly thereafter, large full breasts were seen as beautiful and the height of femininity. In just the next generation, with bras burning across the land, small breasts were "naturally" feminine and those "cursed" with big, full breasts found themselves "too big."

For another hoot, consider how definitions of masculinity and muscularity have changed. Look at George Reeves of the old black-and-white *Superman* TV show. His stomach stuck out beyond his chest; his arms had no noticeably defined muscles. Compare him to Christopher Reeve of the modern *Superman* movies, who was sculpted like a body-builder. Both generations find their models "naturally" manly. Both would find the other's model incomprehensible.

For that matter, you would think at least that cherished staple, the Big Dick, would have a stable cultural identity. I mean, more is always better, right? Not necessarily. Thomas Laqueur[4] relates that the ancient Greeks, from whom we inherit much of our aesthetics, found small penises masculine and attractive. Large dicks were con-sidered animal-like, and often the butt (sorry) of public jokes. Men with big dicks learned shame and began to "tuck," just like any sen-sible drag queen. A transmale friend who recently returned from a trip to Greece told me how comfortable he'd felt. Everywhere he went, all the statues and pictures had small, manly dicks—just like his.

OH YEAH? WELL, MY MOM SAYS YOUR BODY IS JUST A DISCURSIVELY PRODUCED EVENT BASED ON HIGHLY VARIABLE CULTURAL NORMS

As I sat down next to my seatmate on the bus leaving the National Women's Music Festival in Bloomington, Indiana, she said quickly, "Please pardon my fat hips." I was nonplused, not having noticed her hips. Foucault's questions came to mind: What kind of system bids us each make of our bodies a problem to be solved, a claim we must defend, or a secret we must publicly confess, again and again?

Since she and I were stuck together for the next two hours, we proceeded to discuss some of these questions, in particular, why she had felt obliged to apologize to me, a complete stranger.

"Oh, I know, I shouldn't think of them that way," she said. "My feminist friends tell me I should think of them as *nurturing* and *maternal.*"

"Oh, no," I exclaimed, "that's the same thing. It just means this time the jury came back with a different verdict. You're still in the dock awaiting judgment—either way they decide, you'll still have been radically disempowered. The question really should be, what is the original cultural concern with your pelvis and bodyfat that *requires* us to recognize and agree on a meaning in the first place? In other words, whose agenda is it that demands your hips must be gendered with a particular meaning, or to even have any meaning at all?"

"The body," said Simone de Beauvoir, "is a situation."[5] In order to grasp our bodies, to think of them as well as to understand the cultural gaze that fixes upon them, we must construct what our bodies can be said to mean and to look like.

We rely upon other members of our speech community to do this, since it is in the meanings reflected back at us through culture that we find *truth*. Almost everything about bodies is discovered through comparison from the collection of meanings stored in a common language: pretty, fat, plain, masculine, short, light-skinned, wrinkled, feminine, broad, sleek, ugly, athletic, deformed, slim, rotund, buxom, old, delicate. The litany traps and enfolds each body.

For some of us, the meanings culture drapes upon our bodies are extremely painful and depressing. Worse still, a gender system tends to enforce monolithic meanings. Big breasts must mean one thing, hairy backs another, wrinkles yet another still, providing us little or no room to construct our selves and create alternatives.

Simply having our bodies exposed to social judgment can be painful and disturbing to some people. I remember my sixty-five-year-old friend who said, "You know, when I first look at myself in the mirror, I look fine. I think, *Well, all right!* But I look once again, harder, imagining how people must see me, and then I see only the fat and wrinkles and I feel just awful."

What does it cost to tell the truth?

I guess if your sense of self matches closely with the cultural grid of what you should mean, and you find those meanings pleasing, then the "truth" doesn't come too expensive. For the rest of us, though, it can cost a great deal.

---

1. Michel Foucault in *Bodies That Matter: On the Discursive Limits of Sex* by Judith Butler (New York, Routledge, 1993), p. 93.

2. Judith Butler, *Gender Trouble* (New York: Routledge, 1990), p. 114.

3. Kathy Russell, Midge Wilson, and Ronald Hall, *The Color Complex* (New York: Anchor Books, 1992), p. 14.

4. Thomas Laqueur, *Making Sex: Body and Gender from the Greeks to Freud* (Cambridge, MA: Harvard University Press, 1990), p. 31.

5. Simone de Beauvoir, *The Second Sex* (New York: Vintage, 1983), p. 301.

VIDEO TAPE

REWIND

"It's beautiful," I exclaim. It is, in fact, a particularly fine watch my father has just bought for my seventh birthday, the jewelled face throwing back at me the summer's sunlight. "It's...it's...," I hesitate, searching for just the right word, "it's *divine.*" I breathe happily. My father's face comes up sharply, his pupils narrowing. "Boys don't say divine." And he watches me, his head cocked slightly to one side. I open my mouth to question this unfathomable statement, as if certain dictionary words were colored blue for boys and pink for girls, but there is something hard in his voice and eyes. Suddenly, my pleasure evaporates and is replaced entirely by fear. I know if I question him I'll probably get the palm of his hand. You know, when a six-foot-three-inch, two-hundred-pound man hits you in the face with his open hand, it's like being hit in the head with a ham. And so, mumbling something to my feet like, "Well, it is very nice," I make a small mental note to avoid this particular word in the future.

Read at a transexual speak-out held at New York's Lesbian and Gay Community Center in 1993 in honor of the fortieth anniversary of Christine Jorgensen's sex-change surgery.

FAST FORWARD

The woman sitting across from me is so butch she is often mistaken for a man. We have been discussing the pros and cons of her beginning testosterone treatments. But at the moment, she is lecturing me on being more feminine. "You sometimes—I don't want to hurt your feelings—but you sit crosslegged in meetings and sometimes it takes up some of the space of the woman next to you. As a woman, I just wouldn't do that. It's your male training, like the men on the subway who have to spread their legs and take up two seats. You don't understand how intimidating to women male behavior can be."

QUICK REWIND

I have been invited as a guest panelist at the Lesbians Undoing Sexual Taboos conference for women. I sit when I'm done speaking, sensing the pressure that has built up in the room. The women start applauding, and it just goes on and on and on. I sit. I can't even look at this stunning validation, this unbelievable, unsought welcome back into some kind of women's community after I left all that behind twelve years ago in Cleveland. Later, in response to an audience question, I remark how strange it is to be an honored guest at an event that probably would have tossed my ass out ten years ago. It's like riding the crest of a wave. What a strange thing— to be on the edge of a coming change, a change you have waited for, hungered and worked for, that suddenly begins to happen all around you.

FORWARD, NORMAL SPEED

One of the exciting things to come out of the LUST conference is that a woman is planning a dinner and sex party for one hundred women. Oh boy, does this sound hot or what? I've been waiting about a decade for something like this to happen. I find one of the fliers at the Center. As I quickly scan the brochure, I see on the bottom of the last page: *No Men, No Transvestites, and No Transsexuals.* Riding the crest of a wave indeed. The board has just flipped and I have a mouthful of saltwater. For once, I've got to confront someone who is discriminating against me, if only to talk. I call, just asking for a dialogue, a chance to at least explore our differences. After a few minutes she tells me I'm simply a transvestite who has mutilated himself and hangs up.

REWIND

Eighth-grade math class. I cannot hear what the teacher is saying. In fact, I don't care what she's saying. I am totally mesmerized by the sight of Dara Rosen's new young breast disappearing into the cup of her new young bra, something I can just barely see as she sits across from me in her sleeveless dress. Worse, I am torn between wanting desperately to touch that soft breast and wanting desperately to have that soft breast.

FAST FORWARD

I am on the trading floor at Republic National Bank. It is the third day of my nine-month consulting contract. One of the block traders far down the floor is taking down everyone's name and phone extension, and when he gets to me he calls for me to spell out my name. I do, and he yells back, "Riki Anne, that's cute. Where'd that come from?" "Well," I respond, "it used to be Richard." The heads of two distant block traders, intently tracking the DOW movement on their monitors, swivel sharply around as if on soundless ball bearings. They stare briefly at me before returning to the DOW. My boss, sitting next to me, who has come to Wall Street from a very gay twelve-year career in musical theater, chuckles softly without even looking up from his screen. He is having more fun with this than a pig in shit.

FORWARD, NORMAL SPEED

My new boss, a twenty-five-year-old NYU finance graduate, is staring intently at my chest. Actually, not my chest, but the area on my coat over my chest—just over my heart, on the left side. I've been a little intimidated here at J.P. Morgan. I've spent a year and a half trying to get a consulting contract and I'm finally in. I look down, knowing helplessly that I'm probably wearing some of my breakfast. Just what I need. But I am not. What I am wearing is my *Take a Transexual to Lunch* button, which I wear everywhere *but* into work and which this morning, of all mornings, I have neglected to remove.

REWIND

My friend Deborah has offered to stay over with me. It's my first night back home from surgery, and I gratefully accept. We lie quietly in bed together. She's holding me gently. "Can I feel?" she asks after a minute. "Yes, but I have a dilator in, so you can't really go inside." She puts her hand between my legs anyway. "Can I move it?" she asks. "Sure, why not." I have no thought on this subject, just a kind of curiosity and a small, flaming desire to lose whatever kind of virginity this is, after losing so many others. She pushes gently, firmly, on the dilator, as her body leans toward mine. For the first time in my twenty-eight-year-old life, I feel a woman moving inside me, in my vagina.

FAST FORWARD

I am at a private, very underground, lesbian women's S/M night at Paddles here in New York, having been invited by Pat Califia, who, by many accounts, began this movement. This is, at best, a super-marginalized minority within a minority, which New York's Finest can raid with complete impunity at any time they choose during the evening. A woman approaches me, dressed entirely in shining black leather from neck to toe, holding a rather substantial riding crop. She flexes it as we talk. After a few minutes, she confides that she finds me very attractive, and wonders if I enjoy being whipped because she would very much like to whip me. As we continue talking and I mention I am transexual, she freezes, stares intently, and looking a bit green around the gills excuses herself hurriedly to stalk across the room, where she and several of her nontransexual leather-clad lesbian-feminist sado-masochistic (I'm running out of hyphens here) friends can stand and giggle and point at someone as strange and unique as me.

REWIND

Dad is climbing through the fence, which is made of barbed-wire strands, strung from fence posts all over this farm where we are hunting pheasant. It is freezing cold with a half foot of snow on the ground, but we are both bulkily dressed and shod against the weather and the wind that gathers speed blowing down across the open fields. To get through the fence, to separate and hold the rusted barbed wire, he has to hand me his big 12-gauge shotgun, which I hold along with my smaller, lighter 20-gauge. As he climbs through, I can see the only thing around us, the clubhouse, far over his shoulder in the lonely distance, a single black silhouette against the gathering sky. I tell myself I can do it. I can say I dropped it and it went off, and inside my head a little pounding begins and small quivers are starting to knot my stomach and shoulders. You wouldn't really, I say to myself, but already I can see the look of surprise, that final, complete grasp of fact as the shotgun goes off, blowing a hole in that bastard that only a 12-gauge shotgun at very close range can make, a hole I could put my entire thirteen-year-old fist through, the sound echoing off the clubhouse and back at us, locked in that moment, gratefully and mercifully our last moment together. Me knowing I am free, finally, at last. They'll believe me if I cry, if I withdraw into myself. I know how to do months of silent, strained shock to hide from people. He has at least taught me that. And then I imagine the devastation to my mother and our lives, and the years of questions and forms and police and authorities and, while I am thinking of all this, he is through the fence and reaches for me to hand him his gun, no thought in his head but that I obey instantly, as usual, and like a puff of quick air, the single moment of safety and freedom hits me and is gone.

FAST FORWARD

Jaye Davidson is going to pull the trigger. She is absolutely going to pop that nontransexual IRA bitch. I am watching *The Crying Game,* which every nontransexual friend and acquaintance has told me I *must* see, and I'm remembering being in that final presurgical meeting at the Cleveland Clinic. I am in tears, surrounded by about eight doctors and a dozen perky young nurses, trying desperately to convince these sodden bastards that yes, I am a transexual and yes, I want them to make sure I have a functioning clit when they're done carving up my groin because yes, I do still get hot for women and I look forward to them going down on me. One doctor has asked me with barely suppressed disgust how I would feel if I couldn't have an orgasm (how would you feel if your sorry-assed wienie-roasted limp dick couldn't have an orgasm?) and another has pointed to his impossibly feminine, delicate WASP nurse, explaining patiently that I understand, of course, I won't come out looking like *her,* and I am thinking of all the women telling me that I can never be a real woman, presumably like them, and now phrases like *women-born women only, biological women only, genetic women only*—or whatever exclusionary formula is in vogue with our very best lesbian thinkers this year—start tumbling over and over each other in my head like a bunch of manic puppies. I am thinking about all those feminine, self-satisfied, dismissive young Jewish girls I grew up with, went to synagogue with, hated and lusted for and lost sleep over, and I swear I am practically coming in my pants here on the theater seat as Jaye finally pulls the trigger on that nontransexual bitch. Not just once, the first shot echoing out and the surprise registering on those small, delicate, well-spaced features just like I knew it would on my father's larger, heavier European ones. No, Jaye, my hero of the moment, my trans-savior, pulls again and again and again and five, six, seven—how many shots are in an automatic?— until that beautiful nontransexual woman, the kind that if we look like them they tell us how well we pass, she's down for the count, and I'm telling myself frantically after four years of Twelve-Step programs that I'm not about violence and I've given up fighting anyone or anything. But the anger and tears rise in my throat with the bitterness of bile and stick there like some kind of demonic fishbone, and I know helplessly and a little guiltily that I'll rent this video, not for the directing, which is nearly perfect, nor the storyline, which is brilliant, but just to see Jaye pull that trigger in this scene again and again and again.

The problem with transexual women is not that we are trapped in the wrong bodies. The truth is that that is a fairly trivial affair corrected by doctors and sharp scalpels. The problem is that we are trapped in a society which alternates between hating and ignoring, or tolerating and exploiting us and our experience.

More importantly, we are trapped in the wrong minds. We have, too many of us for too long, been trapped in too much self-hate: the hate reflected back at us by others who, unwilling to look at the complexity of our lives, dismiss our femaleness, our femininity, and our sense of gender and erotic choices as merely imitative or simply derivative. Wanting desperately to be accepted, and unable to take on the whole world alone, we have too often listened to these voices that were not our own. We have forgotten what Alice Walker says when she declares:

> *No person is your friend (or kin) who demands your silence, or denies your right to grow and be perceived as fully blossomed as you were intended. Or who belittles in any fashion the gifts you labor so to bring into the world.*[1]

And our lesson is neither new nor unique. From Lyndall MacCowan:

> *It means knowing I'm a freak. It means knowing that I am not a woman. I means falling in love with girls and, at the same time, despising their femininity, their obsession with makeup and boys, their lack of strength and brains. It means knowing that both the kind of woman I want and the kind of woman I am don't exist, do not have names... If it does not someday make me kill myself, it's something that can get me killed.*[2]

Transexuality? No, she's speaking about being a self-identi-fied lesbian femme in the '70s and '80s. There are no new changes, just new faces.

In closing, let me tell you about one transexual. After ten years of hiding and passing and sucking up to nontransexual women, strung out and totally desperate, she started a transexual group.

She started talking with them and hanging out with them and being seen with them, although at first she hated it. She started wearing buttons and coming out at every appropriate and inap-propriate moment, just as if her life were as normal and natural as anyone else's. And she learned that although she might hate herself, she could not hate the fifty or one hundred other transexuals she met, whose stories she heard, whose tears of frustration and rage she saw, whose everyday, one-day-at-a-time, courage to survive she witnessed. And she understood, at last, the redemptive power of community, and how it can only be stifled by self-hate and silence.

Community, my friends and transexual kin is what we build here today, by coming together to claim our own, our history, and our Christine. Christine, standing alone in God's own light, in a way none of us have had to since, made all of this and all of us possible.

---

1. Alice Walker, *In Search of Our Mothers' Gardens* (New York: Harvest/HBJ, 1983), p. 636.

2. Lyndall MacCowan, "Re-collecting History, Renaming Ourselves: Femme Stigma and the Feminist Seventies and Eighties" in *The Persistent Desire: A Femme-Butch Reader*, edited by Joan Nestle (Boston: Alyson, 1992), p. 311.

SEX! IS A VERB

The Transexual Menace demonstrates at a reading Janice Raymond does in 1994 at Judith's Room, the last of New York City's women's bookstores (and now defunct). She is the author of a remarkably hostile, transphobic tract. Dr. Raymond draws about two dozen people who are obviously bewildered to be in the midst of an equal number of genderqueers in black Menace T-shirts. By prior agreement with the owners, Dr. Raymond and I engage in a debate following her reading. I am taken aback as she immediately exclaims, "But why would you want to do that to your body?"

"Do what?" I ask.

"Well, have it cut into, change your sex."

"How do you know I've had surgery?"

"Well, I mean I assume...," she trails off, gesturing vaguely at my Menace T-shirt and looking baffled.

"But why would you care? At the risk of sounding heartless, Dr. Raymond, I don't give a damn what you do with your body."

·

Yes. Hello, I'm a transexual woman and I—

CLICK.

Hello? Hello?

Yes. Hello, I'm interested in changing my sex on my driver's—

CLICK.

Hello? Hello?

MEET ME IN THE DARK, UNDER THE SMALL PART OF THAT CURVE, YOU KNOW—WHERE ALL THE HOT, NEW ANOMALIES HANG OUT

Is there one sex or two? Or, including the intersexed (hermaphrodites), how about three or four? The argument that intersexed bodies are pathology doesn't help us much, because—assuming the bodies are perfectly functional—that's a value judgment masquerading as medical fact.

Saying that the intersexed comprise just a negligible fraction doesn't help us, either. It just takes us out of the land of Fact and Nature, plopping us squarely in the squishy realm of Probabilities and Chance. Deciphering this begins to look suspiciously more like cultural judgment than the cold eye of Impartial Science.

ATTACK OF THE INTERSEXED PEOPLE!

Who gets to say which bodies "count," and why? How small a percentage counts as negligible? Whose body counts as the standard for normal, and how different can I be before I become pathology?

According to the Intersex Society of North America, about one in two thousand births is intersexed. They estimate that five intersexed infants are operated on each day. All these operations, of course, are performed without the patients' consent. Many are mutilated for life by a medical science that seeks to impose aesthetic norms on bodies that function perfectly well but are different. For that matter, forget all these arguments and try the "negligible" line out on Cheryl Chase, a founding member of the protest group Hermaphrodites With Attitude.

HONEST OFFICER, THEY WERE SEXED HERE WHEN I ARRIVED

We're taught that while gender may come from Culture, sex comes from Nature. All bodies already have a sex "in" them. This sex is recognized and expressed by culture as gender through social practices like clothing, hairstyles, and whether one finds pastels simply *faaaaabulous*. In this narrative, sex is a natural property of bodies, while gender is just what culture makes of them. In Judith Butler's terms,[1] Sex is to Nature (raw) as Gender is to Culture (cooked). The naturalness of sex grounds and legitimizes the cultural practices of gender. But what if this narrative is actually inverted?

The more we look, the less natural sex looks. Everywhere we turn, every aspect of sex seems to be saturated with cultural needs and priorities. Mother Nature has Mankind's fingerprints all over Her.

Maybe the formula is reversed. Gender is not what culture creates out of my body's sex; rather, sex is what culture makes when it genders my body. The cultural system of gender looks at my body, creates a narrative of binary difference, and says, "Honest, it was here when I arrived. It's all Mother Nature's doing." The story of a natural sex that justifies gender evaporates, and we see sex standing revealed as an effect of gender, not its cause. Sex, the bodily feature most completely in-the-raw, turns out to be thoroughly cooked, and our comforting distinction between sex and gender collapses. We are left staring once again at the Perpetual Motion Machine of gender as it spins endlessly on and on, creating difference at every turn.

ANOTHER DAY IN THE LIFE OF A GENDERTRASH REJECT

What social systems make the recognition and lifelong attachment of a sex on my body possible? What cultural agencies push it along? Which institutions store and retrieve knowledge about my body, and at what points of contact with society is this information brought into play?

Let's take a walk around town. I've a busy day, so try to keep up. It's 1980 and I'm preparing for "sex-change" surgery, which is wonderful, but the timing is kind of a bummer since I have to register for graduate school at Cleveland State University. But I can handle it. I'm a genderqueer. I can handle anything.

My first stop is the Cleveland Clinic. My social worker makes notes as usual in my chart as I talk about how my life "as a woman" is going, whatever that means. I think it means how people are reacting to me and how I feel about it. But why should that count toward my surgery? I mean, it's going to be my body lying on the table, not theirs, and certainly not the hospital's.

What is it like living as a woman? Well, between the stares in the bathroom with threats to call the cops, and the guys on the street who make sucking noises and comment on the teenage breasts growing on my twenty-six-year-old body, it's no picnic. Everyone seems to be looking at my body and trying to do something about it. She scribbles away.

She asks me to sign these long, legal-looking documents. One says that I understand all the various procedures they're going to do; the other that I'm not married. Seems that after the operation, I'll be considered legally female, so it would be illegal for me to be married. This takes them off the hook. Huh...so if I had a wife, our relationship would suddenly become a same-sex marriage. A loving union made in heaven becomes a crime with a flick of a blade. Oh, goody! She is not amused. I shut up and sign. She gives me a date for surgery.

From the medical bureaucracy to the civil bureaucracy. I go down to the County Recorder's office and don't even get to see a judge. Alas, I will miss the irony of a man who lives half his life running around publicly in a floor-length black dress passing judgment on my gender. Instead I get some bored clerk who looks like a third-year law student. He eyes me sourly from behind a battered gray desk, one of those broad, rough things that invites graffiti. I try to read the desktop art upside down while he examines my proof that I've publicized my legal change of name in the *Cleveland Legal Register* for the required thirty days.

He asks me how the sovereign state of Ohio can know I'm not doing this to defraud someone, because that kind of name change is strictly illegal. *I mean, look at me, asshole. I'm a guy in a dress who gets hassled in the restroom for trying to take a pee and you're worried that I'm going to turn out to be John Freaking Dillinger on the lam in drag? Get a life.* I say nothing, of course, just look at him respectfully and bat my eyelashes until he thinks I'm probably making a pass at him, or the estrogen has fried my brain. He finally signs the papers, staring up at me as if I'm something he's discovered in the back of the fridge from last year's hunting trip.

But I'm not done. I ask him about changing my Ohio birth certificate, which still lists me as male. He loftily informs me that the state of Ohio doesn't do that sort of thing. It turns out they want a record "contemporaneous with my birth." He intones contemporaneous solemnly, all one-hundred-and-twenty-pounds of him. I'd like to contemporaneous his geeky twit head, but right now he's my knight in shining armor because I have my name-change papers tucked under my arm. So, batting my lashes one last time, this time just to cheese him off, I exit stage left. Anyway, it's September, and if I don't get to school in time for registration, all my preferred courses will be closed out.

A guy holds the door for me at the elevator. As he gets in behind me he casually asks, "So, how tall are you anyway, Miss?" Then he looks again, a lot closer. Clearly confused now, he's not sure if he has just been polite or if he's made an ass of himself by holding the door and flirting with a guy in drag.

When I arrive at Cleveland State, I have to fill out the admission forms, including indicating my sex. Well, I guess I can start checking the *F* box. The student behind the counter is trying to be friendly. I've stopped by home to change into a pair of jeans, and he doesn't look real close, thinks he's talking to the average guy, and asks, "You play any hoops?" As I consider the answer he eyes the forms I've been completing, spots *Sex: F,* and looks up quickly. But by then he's mine. "Oh yeah. Love to. In the men's league last year they considered me just a small forward. But in the women's league this year I got to play a Patrick Ewing sort of power center."

"Great," he replies, without an ounce of enthusiasm. I want to ask him if we can go out and shoot baskets sometime, but he's already turning an interesting shade of green so I leave for the registration lines. On the way I stop to sign up for student insurance, which they offer at a really good discount. Again I have to declare and sign my sex. Only this time, I have to answer a whole barrage of questions: Have I ever been pregnant? Hmmm...let me think. Have I ever had an abortion? Not knowingly. Do I need information on birth control pills? Not unless my surgeon is a lot better than I think he is. But who knows, a good girl scout is always prepared. I check that one *Yes*. Maybe now I'll find out where you insert those little pink pills.

It's on the way to the financial aid office that I become aware I have to pee. This is always the most complex part of the day. Getting a sex-change is easier than negotiating the public toilet system. Which is worse—a woman in the men's room in heels using the urinal, or a man in the women's room using a stall? It's a toss-up. I make a beeline for the women's room.

Naturally, there's a line. I have to stand there, pretending ignorance of all the stares. Although half the women waiting are more butch and gender-variant than I am, I'm a head taller than anyone else. What can I say—a swan among the platypuses draws attention.

Someone asks me the time, which is usually a voice check. I see that she is wearing a watch herself. She's closely examining my face, along with about three of her friends. The rest of the line is casually watching while trying to look like they're not watching. I'm tempted to shift into low gear here and use my truckdrivin' growl, but I need a stall, not a scene. I answer in my highest and most petite voice. They ain't convinced, but at least they conclude I'm not the Mad Cleveland Bathroom Rapist stalking their restroom.

Once in the cubicle, I sit. But then I notice I'm making more noise than anyone else. They're all swooshing, and I'm splashing like a fire hose against a kettle drum at close range. I pass on fluffing before the mirror when I'm done and beat a hasty retreat. Discretion is the better part of gender valor. On my way out, a dyke smiles indulgently. Mon ami!

At the student aid office there are still more forms for loans, for the minimum-wage on-campus job they're throwing in to sweeten the package, and for more insurance in case I croak in school so the loan is retired. Each time I have to record and declare my sex. Why do they need my sex on a loan, for chrissakes? Do penises pay differently? Am I going to sit on the money or something so that what's between my legs makes a difference? When I have a vagina will they change my interest rate?

The registration lines still reach halfway across the gym. But, in short order, I'm done. It's almost five o'clock and time to go. I stop off at the library for some books I'll need for the first day of classes. Too much Coke while waiting in lines and again I need a bathroom.

Uh-oh. This time there are two CSU campus cops in their brown uniforms right outside the door. This is a city campus, and they're fully armed these days. The whole thing flashes in my mind like an old George Raft movie:

> Cop One: "All right, Miss, step away from that door!"
>
> Cop Two: "Look out, Charlie! She's got a dick!"
>
> Cop One: "Don't move, Miss! Okay, put both balls on top of your head. Now lay your dick on the floor, and kick it over here...slowly!"

I can't handle another situation right now. I need to get busted for Public Impersonating like I need a hemorrhoid. I'll bear the pain until I get home. A young kid on the subway, noticing I'm carrying a load of books, offers me his seat. Chivalry isn't dead. Then his friend elbows him and whispers and they both look at me again and start to crack up. Chivalry hits the floor, colder'n a mackerel.

That's the easy part. The hard stuff is getting past the guys hanging around the corner near my house. It's usually not too bad, only they don't seem to know my name. One of them thinks I'm someone called "Mary Cohen." No, wait, it's *maricon*. Another calls me *putah*. They do this every time I walk by. So far nothing physical has come of it, but I'm waiting and I'm also well-prepared. I'm well-prepared to hysterically cry my head off the first time one of them so much as touches me; then I'll hit them with a full load of Jewish guilt. After that, they won't want to live.

I have a date tonight with Kris, my sweetheart. Contemplating this makes the day behind much more bearable. She comes by at eight, and we go to our favorite gay bar. The music is awesome. While I get up to snag some brewskies, another woman comes up to her and says, "You know, that's really a guy you're with."

Kris just smiles sweetly. As if mulling over this new information, she begins thoughtfully scratching her chin with her middle finger. Later that night she wonders aloud if my surgery will "finally make an honest lesbian of me." Who knows? What are labels, anyway, but whole-body condoms to protect us from making intimate contact with each other?

WHAT IF THEY GAVE A SEX AND NOBODY CAME?

Sex! is a cultural command that all bodies understand and recognize themselves in a specific way, an identification of our bodies that we are forced to carry around and produce on demand. To participate in society, we must be sexed.

We see this with perfect clarity in the case of the intersexed, the original lost brigade in any discussion of binary sex. Intersexuals are not permitted to live without a sex. Even if they resist, society inevitably forces one on them. The machinery of sex gets very upset when you try to live outside of it.

I have a friend who is raising his first child. He is determined to raise it without a sex until it is old enough to select its own. In the meantime, he tells me he cannot believe the incredible intensity of the daily cultural pressure he gets to sex his child. From the person at the checkout counter who asks, "Is that a boy or a girl?" to the insistent hospital records office which absolutely requires a sex, to salespeople in the kiddy clothing stores, to the forthcoming battles with nursery school officials.

There is an entire social apparatus whose sole purpose is to determine, track, and maintain my sex. Perhaps sex is not a noun at all. Perhaps it is really a verb, a cultural imperative—as in, "Sex yourself!"—in the face of which none of us has a choice.

---

1. Judith Butler, *Gender Trouble* (New York: Routledge, 1990), p. 37.

THE MENACE
STATEMENT
TO JANICE RAYMOND

ON BEHALF OF THE MENACE AND FRIENDS, I'd like to thank you and Judith's Room for this time and opportunity for dialogue.

I'd like to begin by addressing some of the tenets of your book, *The Transsexual Empire: The Making of a She-Male.*[1] To begin with, your uncritical invocation of a category of "woman" assumes a fact not in evidence: that there exists a universal and immutable, ahistorical, and unproblematic class called "women," unsullied by definitional, biological, or cultural diversity. The notion that there is an innate essence to "woman," i.e., that a woman in Borneo perceives and constructs her womanhood, experience, and oppression in precisely the same way as a white suburban housewife in Shaker Heights, Ohio, or even in the same way as my Italian female-to-male transsexual friend, Nick Gianelli, is theoretically and factually indefensible. It reenacts that familiar imperialistic arrogance which seeks

Statement read in the winter of 1994 during a confrontation/debate between Dr. Janice Raymond and members of the New York City chapter of the Transsexual Menace. The debate was held at the women's bookstore Judith's Room, and was made possible through the efforts of owners Sally Owen and Carole Levin, as well as through the kind permission of Dr. Raymond.

to submit all cultures and experience to western norms.

Your attempt to rest gender categories upon a biological foundation is similarly indefensible. Within the category of those living as "women" are infertile women, women without wombs, women without breasts, women with XY chromosomes, women whose blood flows primarily with testosterone, hermaphroditic women, intersexed women with both genitals, transgendered women, stone butches and diesel dykes, passing women, incredibly hot drag kings, female-to-male preoperative transexuals, and even gendertrash rejects like me. When you arrogate to yourself the work of policing the borders of this diverse class, you reinstitute the very strictures of coercion and control, of exclusion and limitation, that feminism seeks to overthrow.

Moreover, just as feminists have charged that patriarchy made women's bodies a site of contested meaning, and then appropriated women's flesh and experience as a tabula rasa upon which to inscribe their constructions of a subordinated Other, just so, you have made of our bodies a site of contested meaning, and then appropriated transexual flesh and experience as a tabula rasa upon which to inscribe your constructions of us as subordinated Other. Once again you are reenacting the very oppressive mechanisms from which feminism is seeking emancipation.

Finally, as we look more deeply into not just the history of women, but the history of the category of "women," we can ask what the political stakes in creating and enforcing false and simplistic dichotomies like male/female, man/woman, and masculine/feminine are. It has become increasingly apparent that these binary structures benefit a presumptive and compulsive heterosexual economy. Heterosexism requires binary and opposing sexes and genders: if there were a hundred genders, "heterosexuality" could not exist.

If desire could finally free itself, as it continues to do within our queer community, it would have little use for rigid categories to contain its erotic expression or channel its hunger toward an acceptable, opposing, and procreative gender. The unstructured multiplicity, the sheer creativity of queer genders strike at the very foundations of heterosexuality, and this is exactly why queers have historically been targets for straight prejudice, bashing, and outright hatred. Again, when you reify gender roles into neat binary boxes, when you invest yourself to keep barbarians like me from the gates, you become an agent of the very oppressions we as queers seek to confound and overturn.

I'd like to end with a few personal notes:

You say we want to "pass" as women. Well, I don't pass. I wear this Transexual Menace logo every place I go. Between the two of us, only you pass as a woman. If, as de Beauvoir held, "One is not born a woman, but becomes one," if femininity is an invention of men foisted on women, if feminine behavior is a learned cultural performance of hair, clothing, voice, gesture, and stance so one is perceived as a female, then by presenting yourself as a woman it is you who have been co-opted into traditional sex roles, you who serve their institutions, and you who are performing here.

In spite of this, I want you to know that I will respect and even defend your right to call yourself a woman this evening.

When I first heard of *The Transsexual Empire* I thought, "What an empowering title. At last a book for me." Just what I needed after having been dispossessed of my lover of seven years, my family, my job, my apartment building, and most of my friends. It was not what I needed, however, and after reading it I wept for several days. It dismissed my courage and resourcefulness, it denigrated the complexity of my identity, it ridiculed my struggles. With your facile comparisons to Nazi medical experiments, your malicious assessments of our masochistic desire for pain, and your derisive slurs on our sanity, you have caused immeasurable pain to my community and the people I love.

It was only a few months ago, responding to a party invitation at the Gay Community Center, that I neglected to read the footnote: *No Transvestites, No Men, and No Transexuals.* When I called the lesbian in charge she told me I was really just a transvestite who had mutilated himself and hung up on me.

Ideas have effects. It is clear that as transgendered men and women, we face two kinds of violence each day. One is the larger violence, that perpetrated by straight society on our bodies. It has taken from us people like Brandon Teena and Marsha P. Johnson. We recall that before he was shot in the back of the head, Brandon was repeatedly raped by two men bent on demonstrating to his girlfriend that he was "really a woman." Ideas have effects.

Unfortunately, deaths like Brandon's and Marsha's are just additional bricks in the wall, a bloody and unspeakable wall, one held together by the caked and ugly mortar of transphobia, built one brick at a time in the silence and darkness of our invisibility. And this invisibility is facilitated by the smaller violence, that perpetrated by writers and theorists like you who, by their insistence that our men are really women, or that our women are really men, or that we are crazed masochistic he-shes, or self-mutilating cross-dressed she-males, serve to lend the genderbashing of transexual men and women a social, and respectable, face to show the world.

If you turn over the little boxes into which you want to put us, Ms. Raymond, or from which you so want to evict us, you'll see they're all stamped *Made in Patriarchy.* And look at the shipping label. It reads *All Proceeds Go to Benefit Heterosexuality.* Little boxes are for things, not people; and guarding little boxes is the task of fools.

Now look around you at the transexual and transgendered faces here tonight, at the dignity and survival written in these faces. Let me assure you: We are more complex than your theories, more creative than your dogma, and much more stubborn and rude and resourceful than your politics.

Thank you again for your time.

---

1. Janice Raymond, *The Transsexual Empire: The Making of a She-Male* (Boston: Beacon, 1979).

Birth of the Homosexual

"How do you know you want rhinoplasty, a nose job?" he inquires, fixing me with a penetrating stare.

"Because," I reply, suddenly unable to raise my eyes above his brown wingtips, "I've always felt like a small-nosed woman trapped in a large-nosed body."

"And how long have you felt this way?" He leans forward, sounding as if he knows the answer and needs only to hear the words.

"Oh, since I was five or six, doctor, practically all my life."

"Then you have a rhino-identity disorder," the shoetops state flatly. My body sags in relief. "But first," he goes on, "we want you to get letters from two psychiatrists and live as a small-nosed woman for three years...just to be sure."

Round Up the Usual Suspects

How can a transexual woman know she's a lesbian? How can any woman know she's a lesbian? For that matter, how did I know I was transexual? I remember being very confused and wanting to do rather dreadful things to my body and gender display, then reading Christine Jorgensen's book[1] and thinking, *That's it, that's what I must be. I'm a transexual.* Borrowing from Marjorie Garber,[2] my nose job was something I did, but my dick job was something I was. Having a dick job meant acquiring a whole new identity. Loving my girlfriend meant I was now a lesbian. I had become a transexual, and I was in someone else's body.

It is doubtless the case that since humans walked upright, they have engaged in certain sexual practices that are, well, disgusting. These include—persons of delicate sensibility may want to skip this part—licking each other's genitals, inserting things into each other's anuses, and various acts of such a perverse nature even I can't bring myself to enumerate them here.

For a man in ancient Greece, taking another man's penis in his mouth or anus was not considered a gendered act reserved for female bodies. The idea that acts of pleasure, or where you parked your genitals for the evening, could and ought to constitute a sensible basis for your primary social identity would have been amusing to them, if not absurd.

At various other times and in various other cultures, of course, these were fully gendered acts, and two male bodies performing them were engaged in sodomy. The category could also include sex with animals, whether consenting or not, with or without leather accoutrement.

As cultural power turned itself to the practice of pleasure, determined to control and bring it into alignment with various norms, an ever stricter system of classification was introduced. This was done, as usual, in the name of Science, and with our usual confidence that more knowledge was a good thing. Science demanded that the most commonplace, as well as the most obscure, sexual practices come forward, plead their case and be evaluated, judged, and classified.

This was not a case of more and better science. Please don't tax me by maintaining that science was unaware of all the various practices of pleasure. Nor does it seem likely that this constituted the outraged reaction of an innocent and naive science which was shocked (shocked!) to discover homosexual conduct in its midst.

AND OVER HERE, OUR NEWEST INVENTION: THE HOMOSEXUAL

It was, Michel Foucault says, in the nineteenth century that the "homosexual became a personage, a past, a case history, and a childhood, in addition to being a type of life....The sodomite had been a temporary aberration; the homosexual was now a species."[3]

Foucault underlined the distinction between the productive and negative effects of power. We think of cultural power as primarily restraining, punishing, and repressing homosexuals. Yet a discussion which places "the homosexual" as its starting point is unable to look back at how that same power actually produced "the homosexual" in the first place, the very same homosexual it is then said to repress.

In this way, our consistent preoccupation with a narrative of a cultural power which is only restrictive succeeds in hiding and legitimizing its most profound productive effect: creating the separate social identity of the homosexual.

All this was not limited to homosexuals. Other perverts were produced in abundance. For instance, if you are turned on by older bodies, you are a gerontophiliac, unless, presumably, you are in your eighties, in which case you're normal. Similarly, if you're sexually aroused by fourteen-year-old boys, you're a pedophile, unless you're a fourteen-year-old girl, in which case you're normal. If you exchange heated looks with Max, your German shepherd, you're a zoophile. And by the mid-1900s, when medical technology made it possible, if you wanted hormones and a dick job, you had a mental disease called Gender Identity Disorder and were a transexual (genitophile?).

In addition, the category of *homosexual,* which created an entire identity around the satisfaction of erotic or romantic desire, made no sense whatsoever without first creating a *heterosexual* with whom he or she could be compared. While this point is overlooked by Foucault, it is exploited in gleeful detail by Jonathan Ned Katz in *The Invention of Heterosexuality.*[4]

In this spirit, Judith Butler argues that a "homosexual revolution"[5] which hopes to overturn heterosexuality is paradoxically self-defeating since it will actually require that very heterosexuality. Furthermore, by ignoring the productive effects of power, it will also unconsciously succeed in enshrining the parochial nineteenth-century notion that how one gets off in bed should form the basis for one's social identity.

It is easy to maintain that all this is just a simple matter of naming, or, if you prefer, misnaming. Not so. Everyday speech is conducted according to a largely implicit set of universal givens that everyone within a common speech community accepts. These givens act as rules, enabling us to interpret what statements mean, even what things can be said. Because these rules are common to all members of this community, more or less, they form a powerful basis for each of us to construct and experience the reality of our bodies. This is why it is so difficult and frustrating to say anything useful about transgendered or intersexed (hermaphroditic) bodies. The rules of the discourse actually prevent intelligent communication.

HOMOSEXUALITY: ONCE MORE INTO THE BREECHES

This reminds me of a lesbian friend who became quite upset because she was dating a male transexual. Only twenty-four, she had come out just three years before and found being an out lesbian one of the most powerful experiences of her life.

Yet, when she was walking down the street with this now-bearded young man, arm-in-arm, she found herself suddenly being read as your average straight white woman. She had become invisible as a lesbian and she hated it, even to the point of considering breaking up—in spite of the fact that in bed there were still two very active vaginas, you might say, on hand.

Labels like *homosexual* are not just some passing scientific categories, the mistakes of an over-eager taxonomist. They find their way into formal social structures such as science, law, medicine, and psychology, and also into a wide array of informal social structures: from the guy who yells *faggot* on the street, to the friends who pressure you to take a date to the prom, to the murderous nelly queen who dies horribly at the end of the movie, to the cops who casually roust your bar.

All these structures Foucault called *juridical*. They are pervasive and very powerful, even though only some of them are inscribed in books of law, medicine, and science. What may have started out as descriptive labels used by Kraft-Ebbing and Havelock Ellis end up as real, political categories. Just ask anyone labeled a homosexual during the Vietnam-era draft.

The discourse on "the homosexual," along with the corresponding array of juridical structures, produces the ways in which people who engage in same-sex pleasures understand themselves. Like my lesbian friend, they actually begin to experience themselves in and through a label which didn't exist until a hundred years ago.

PLANT A HOMOSEXUAL, GROW A HOMOSEXUAL MOVEMENT

This is why I am at pains to point out, wherever I speak, that I am not a transexual, nor am I interested in a transgender rights movement, one which, unable to interrogate the fact of its own existence, will merely end up cementing the idea of a binary sex which I am presumed to somehow transgress or merely traverse.

This is also why I am deeply uncomfortable when transpeople tell me glowing tales about how revered the Native American berdache was: transpeople as gifted shamans. I don't want to bear the burden of being especially good any more than I want to bear that of being especially bad. Both inscribe my identity in ways which take it out of my hands.

While I recognize how important it is to produce histories and sociologies of transpeople, I am wary of anything that might cement the category more firmly in place. I'd also like us to investigate the means by which categories like *transgender* are produced, maintained, and inflicted on people like me. It's not so much that there have always been transgendered people; it's that there have always been cultures which imposed regimes of gender. It is only within a system of gender oppression that transgender exists in the first place. It would be impossible to transgress gender rules without the prior imposition of those rules. Studying transgender (or for that matter, homosexuality) by itself risks essentializing the category and, at the same time, naturalizing the gender regimes that install it and the "normal" gender displays that go unregulated.

In the same vein, I'm often ambivalent about the Great People school of Gay Pride. It is as ridiculous to ask me to feel better about myself because Leonardo da Vinci sucked cock as it is for a straight-identified person to feel better because Picasso ate cunt. Filling in the erasures and silences of hetero-centric history is important, but does anyone believe Leonardo built his identity on whom he fucked, or even considered himself a homosexual? Did he think of himself as queer in the same way that, say, Harvey Fierstein does? Does this not smack of the same kind of monolithic cultural imperialism we deplore?

For identities like gay or lesbian or transgender to be visible and distinct, how many other complex and unnamed identities have to be silenced and erased? Does the gay, lesbian, bisexual, and transgendered movement's noun-list approach really solve anything? Or do we add to it each minority the dominant culture names next so it can regulate and stigmatize it?

It is not enough to have pride in our identities, or to be inclusive. It is time for us to start looking upstream and questioning how these identities were produced. How does homosexual identity actually require an antecedent heterosexuality? Does an identity based on sexual or affectional or gendered practice make any rational sense? Does not our willingness to inhabit queer identities legitimize the notion that every body ought to be socially defined by its potential contribution to procreation?

I will defend anyone's wish to call themselves drag, transexual, transgender, gay, bi, tri, or quad. For me, these are not natural identities but simply political categories we are forced to inhabit when we do certain things with our bodies. And it is my larger agenda to fight this cultural machinery which categorizes, stigmatizes, and then marginalizes minorities, rather than to fight for the rights of one particular category over another.

ALL OF US ARE QUEER

It is arguably the case that when the message of gay liberation changed from *All People Are Queer* to *Gay Is as Good as Straight*, the movement lost its revolutionary potential, its moral and redemptive center. It ceded to the very oppressive system it formed to contest the terms of its struggle and allowed the system to dictate the terms of its resistance.

In effect, at that moment, the heterosexual imperative had already won on the largest issue: gay liberation would not engage a radical freeing of sexuality, nor a reformulation of the orders of desire. It would, instead, merely seek to architect itself into the prevailing regime, largely accepting that regime's values, leaving unquestioned and unchallenged the larger social agenda of marking bodies by the object of their desire, of making affectional or romantic attraction a foundational premise for identity.

Gay liberation has increasingly focused on mainstream acceptance which will gain for acceptable queers full civil rights, while largely bypassing the issues of those queerer queers who might upset the civil rights apple cart by distressing the straight power structure. Gay liberation would more and more be about "normal" family life, children, white people, and good teeth. It would never again be about black drag queens, transexual gendertrash, nelly queers, and diesel dykes.

It would no longer seek to challenge cultural imperatives of normalcy. Even less would it seek to loudly and boldly contest society's continuous crusade to marginalize and deprive those most vulnerable of its subjects as a punishment for being found "abnormal" or "deviant." It would simply attempt to place the few acceptable queers within the prevailing definitions of normalcy.

You see this in the approaches of national gay groups, which appear less interested in the diversity of our community, or the intersection of oppressions which meet in our complex lives and bodies, than in forwarding a narrow-band gay rights agenda. The mainly young, straight-looking, middle-class posterkids they seem to have adopted as the gay face we will show the world look indistinguishable from the adverts for Young Americans for Freedom or even Up with People.

Doubtless, for their aims, this is political pragmatism. But while politics may be the art of the possible, people and movements are not driven by pragmatics. They are driven by inspiration, by vision, by daring, even by desperation. For the past decade, the gay rights movement has consistently failed to articulate any larger vision of social change than *We Want Our Rights.*

This is not a very edifying message. The last best strategy of every movement is a rights-based struggle whose heartbeat is no more or less than a stripped-down appeal to enlightened self-interest.

You hope that there are other voices, that there are those of us who remember that gay liberation was started by Third World queers of color, stone butches, transexuals, and other gendertrash like Sylvia Rivera, Yvonne Ritter, and Marsha Johnson. They were in the Stonewall Inn that night because their lives intersected so many kinds of oppression that they had no place else to go. These were people who, when the police batons started raining down on their heads, did not say, "We're only doing this for gay rights."

I hope there are those of us who remember that a gay liberation movement was first and foremost about the radical, redemptive, and even transformative power of love to change the world. And by love, I do not just mean the easy love for friends, family, or lovers. I mean the hard love, the impossible love for those who hate and fear us and sometimes want to do us harm.

I hope, too, that there are those of us who remember that if that often absent and most unmentioned of queers—God herself—meant for us to learn anything from the journey through this particular kind of life, it is the experience of outsiderdom, and how the suppression of difference has the power to kill hearts and minds and even lives.

Perhaps a gay rights movement will be sufficient to change the whole structure. It is, doubtless, much better than nothing, and a worthwhile goal for many. At the same time I cannot escape the nagging suspicion that gay liberation has disregarded Audre Lorde's oft-quoted dictum that "the master's tools will never dismantle the master's house,"[6] and has, instead, contented itself with simply building a small, yet tastefully furnished addition out back.

1. Christine Jorgensen, *Christine Jorgensen: A Personal Autobiography* (New York: Bantam, 1968).

2. Marjorie Garber, *Vested Interests: Cross-Dressing and Cultural Anxiety* (New York: Harper Perennial, 1993), p. 117.

3. Michel Foucault, *The History of Sexuality: An Introduction,* vol. 1 (New York: Vintage, 1990), p. 43.

4. Jonathan Ned Katz, *The Invention of Heterosexuality* (New York: Dutton, 1995).

5. Judith Butler, *Gender Trouble* (New York: Routledge, 1990), p. 128.

6. Audre Lorde, "The Master's Tools Will Never Dismantle the Master's House" in *This Bridge Called My Back: Writings by Radical Women of Color,* edited by Gloria Anzáldua and Cherríe Moraga (New York: Kitchen Table: Women of Color Press, 1983), p. 98.

THE GAY GAMES
CONTROVERSY

IN 1994, A UNIQUE CONFLUENCE OF EVENTS took place in New York City. For the first time, the Gay Games—our queer Olympics—was held there, with competitions scheduled for a number of high-profile venues, including Yankee Stadium. There was even a fundraiser slated for Madison Square Garden. All of this was happening during the same week as the twenty-fifth-anniversary celebration of the Stonewall Riot, the event that launched the gay liberation movement.

A transexual woman, seeking to participate, tried to sign up for the Gay Games. Although she clearly identified herself, she was repeatedly addressed as "Sir" and read the following rules from the Gay Games registration book regarding all "transitioning individuals," interpreted to mean *all* transexuals:

- Supply a letter from your personal physician confirming you have been on hormones for at least eighteen months.

- Supply a letter from your personal physician attesting to your health.

- Supply a letter from your personal therapist confirming that you have been in therapy for at least eighteen months.

- Supply a letter from your personal therapist explaining why it would be "impossible or detrimental" for you to compete in your "birth sex."

She was told she would probably have to compete as a man, and could compete openly and without requirements if she agreed to do so.

Needless to say, the Transexual Menace was unamused. We began to leaflet Gay Games activities. One of the first people given our flier happened to be Ann Northrop, a member of the Gay Games board. Shortly thereafter she called to invite us to address the board, and asked us to write a statement of our position.

Representatives from the Transexual Menace, TransGender Rights!, and the Metropolitan Gender Network attended the board meeting. The board first tried to say the rules were only meant for pre-operative transexuals. We responded that if that was the case, for purposes of the Gay Games we were all pre-op. No one would register as post-op and, in any case, it was no one's business what was in our pants. Friendly, if heated, discussion ensued for over an hour.

The Gay Games leadership courageously took the high road, for several days later Ann called to say the policy had been overturned. The one we advocated was substantially accepted, and a national public announcement followed. Although she has never claimed credit for it, I suspect much of this was due to Ann's behind-the-scenes work. Also important was the brave intercession of board member Andrew Velez, who said something like, *We have a responsibility here and, although we're going to take some heat, we need to exercise it. We haven't been radical enough.*

The statement we submitted follows:

March 12, 1994

Ms. Ann Northrop
c/o The Gay Games
New York, New York

Ms. Ann Northrop:

Pursuant to our conversations last week, the following contains: (A) our objections to the current requirements for transexual/transgender participation in the Gay Games; (B) our suggestion for its replacement if a statement on transexual/transgender participation is absolutely necessary; and (C) our goals in our continuing actions against the Games' restrictive and offensive policies.

A. Our objections to the current requirements:

> 1. They were arrived at without the knowledge, participation, or consent of transgender/transexual people, and are subsequently being imposed upon us by nontransexuals.

> 2. Gay Games does not currently screen other participants for height, weight, or strength requirements.

> 3. Although a statistical percentage of nontransexual women are chromosomally XY, Gay Games does not currently screen for this.

> 4. Although a statistical percentage of nontransexual women have elevated levels of testosterone, Gay Games does not currently screen for this.

> 5. The requirements are unduly restrictive and, among all the diverse groups competing in the Games, succeed in uniquely stigmatizing transgender/transexual people.

> 6. They place an undue burden upon us to violate the privacy of our relationships with our physicians and therapists.

7. The requirement that we must provide a letter from our personal therapist (we all have them, of course) explaining why it would be "impossible or detrimental" to compete in our birth sex, is so breathtakingly transphobic and offensive as to beggar description. How would Gay Games like it if an Olympic athlete wanted to compete as openly gay, and the U.S. Olympics Committee required a letter from their personal therapist (you all have them, of course) explaining why it would be "impossible or detrimental" for them to compete as straight?

8. It is not your, or anyone's, business what is in our pants, how it got there, or how long it's going to be there. Nor is it our business what's in yours, although we are confident it's thoroughly delightful. If, on the other hand, Gay Games would care to institute a universal panty check of all participants, I will personally volunteer to check all women seeking to enter the Games (it's dirty work, but somebody's got to do it).

9. The requirements, euphemistically referring to an undefined class called "transitioning individuals," are being applied across the board to all transgendered and transexual persons seeking registration. This has included those of us who are pre-operative, those of us who are post-transition, and those of us who are anywhere from two-to-fourteen years post-operative.

10. Relief or appeal from the requirements is done by soliciting an undefined group of individuals which, I am fairly confident, contains not a single transexual or transgendered person among them. (Didn't any of you see the Anita Hill hearings? You know: dignified African-American woman, panel composed entirely of straight white males sitting in judgment on her experience... that sort of thing.)

11. The current requirements being imposed upon us are demeaning in their inception, invasive in their application, and arbitrary in their scope.

12. They suck.

B. Our suggestion for replacement of the current requirements, if a statement of some kind is necessary (which we believe is not the case):

"Transgendered and transexual individuals are welcome to compete in the Gay Games, and are encouraged to do so in the sex role in which they live their normal daily lives."

C. Our goals in our continuing actions against the Gay Games policies:

1. Removal of *all* current requirements relating to our participation in the Gay Games.

2. Public announcement of the requirements removal, press releases stating the same sent to all periodicals and media sources with which Gay Games regularly deals, and further good-faith efforts to alert transgendered and transexual persons who were discouraged and/or prevented from registering in the past.

3. Extension of the deadline for registration to an additional thirty days after the public announcement and press releases. This is to allow sufficient time for transgendered and transexual persons, who were discouraged and/or prevented from signing up, to register for the Games.

4. Reprinting the current Gay Games registration pamphlet, or, failing that, a notice of policy change inserted into all copies from this date forth.

5. Sensitivity training for individuals working at Gay Games by transexual/transgendered persons. This includes training for those who, in the past, have continually referred to clearly identified transexual women seeking registration as *Sir, Mister,* and *He.*

6. Pursuant to the sensitivity training, the hiring of at least two transexual/transgendered persons to work at Gay Games until their completion.

7. A meeting between the Gay Games board and the transexual/transgender community to: (a) air our grievances; (b) open lines of communication (so you need never again go in search of the mythical nontransexual "expert in transexuality": you can feel entirely comfortable talking to us about us); (c) prevent future occurrences and/or friction; and (d) underline the historical and continuing contributions by transexual and transgendered people to the queer community and struggle.

Until our goals have been met in full, we will continue our public protests, education, and actions against the Games' policies up to, and including, the Games themselves. We do this more in a spirit of regret than antagonism. In spite of the Games' demonstrated indifference to our contributions to the queer community, we are aware of the enormous effort, talent, and desire which have gone into the Games.

Nonetheless, we are not prepared to be doormats for anyone, nor to be marginalized in any way, nor to have our concerns or participation sacrificed for anyone else's comfort. In other words: *We're here. We're queerer. Get used to it.* See you at the Games. Inside or, if need be, outside.

Yours in queerness,

Riki Anne Wilchins
Transexual Menace

WHY IDENTITY POLITICS
REALLY, REALLY SUCKS

An attendee at NOW's Young Feminists Conference, when asked about the horrific incidence of men's prison rape, is heard to say, "NOW is about women, not men." A second attendee responds, "But if you're against sexual violence, what possible difference could it make what's between the victim's legs?"

The Human Rights Campaign introduces an Employment Non-discrimination Bill (ENDA) which deliberately excludes protection for gender expression because, as one staffer privately alleges, "It would cost us twenty votes." Transpeople picket in two dozen cities. When HRC's Executive Director brings the principal organizers to their D.C. headquarters, her opening question is, "Why come after us? Why not pick on someone else?" One of the organizers yells back, "No! The moral question isn't, 'Why come after us?' It's, 'Why did we have to?'"

A member of GenderPAC, the national organization founded by transpeople, "devoted to gender, affectional, and racial equality," says, "Of course race and class are important, but we can't devote

too much time to them. They aren't our issues." A second member
points out, "But isn't the we *that defines our issues white, middle*
class, and employed?"

In Washington, D.C., an EMS technician stops treating a critically
injured black woman following a hit-and-run when he cuts open
her pants to discover a penis. Backing away, he then begins making
jokes to the horrified crowd. Dawn Wilson, a former NAACP board
member, writes an impassioned letter to her organization, implor-
ing them to speak out. She receives a pro forma letter stating that of
course the incident is terrible, but the "NAACP is about racism, not
gender expression."

A staffer at the White House Liaison Office for Gay and Lesbian
Affairs turns down a request by transpeople for a meeting to discuss
trans-inclusion in pending hate crimes legislation, stating, "But you
aren't gays and lesbians."

ONE MORE TIME, FROM THE TOP

Okay, please raise your hand if you still think identity politics works.

Whenever I'm invited to address a queer audience, inevitably someone asks, "But why transgender? I thought Gay Lib was about sexual orientation, not gender." I always reply, "Excuse me? Are you telling me that inserting a man's penis into your body is not a fully gendered act, regulated and reserved for only female bodies?"

But this voice that asks, "Aren't we about sexual orientation?" fails to amaze; eventually, it fails even to surprise. It is the same voice that says, "We're about sexual orientation, not racism." Which is true, unless you're African American and queer, or Asian and queer, or Latina and queer, or Native American and queer. It says, "We're about sexual orientation, not class." Which is true, unless you're a queen trying to survive on welfare. And it says, "We're about sexual orientation, not gender." Which is true, unless you're a trans or bisexual or lesbian woman concerned about the right to choose, about spousal abuse, about the freedom to walk our streets without the crippling specter of rape. And, as churches go up in flames around the country, I hope that at least you and I are clever enough to know that surely *this* is not a gay issue. Which it isn't, until the torches come for the Metropolitan Community Church, Beth Simcat Torah, or Unity Fellowship Church.

There is a common cultural machinery at work, and its tools are fearfully similar from one group to the next. It defines and stigmatizes them. It pushes them out to the margins. And then it flushes them out the bottom economically. You can't change that system by just getting your own rights, tinkering with the engine and leaving. You have to take on the whole machine.

ALL OF THE REAL WOMEN, TAKE A SEAT—THE REST OF YOU CAN LEAVE

The head of New York City NOW, the oldest and largest chapter, informs me that I am welcome, but only to work on "women's" issues. I cannot work on my own, which, by definition, are "men's" issues. "Do you mean I can work on your access to postmenopausal hormones, but not on my access to pretransition hormones?" I ask. "Your breast implants after mastectomy but not my breast implants before sex-change? Your danger of ovarian cancer but not my danger of prostate cancer?" She nods, glaring steadily. On the way out she asks me for a hug.

Feminist politics begins with the rather commonsense notion that there exists a group of people understood as *women* whose needs can be politically represented and whose objectives sought through unified action. A movement for women—what could be simpler? But implicit in this is the basic idea that we know who comprises this group since it is their political goals we will articulate. What if this ostensibly simple assumption isn't true?

For starters, we'll have to decide who qualifies as a woman for inclusion in our movement. Otherwise, we'll find ourselves representing anybody who calls themselves a woman. Now, we know that we don't want transexual women: just taking hormones and having a vagina made doesn't make you a woman. We don't want transexual men either: they're busy taking hormones, getting hairy chests, and becoming, well...men. We can't have too many stone butches, diesel dykes, or passing women, because they all live as men. What could they know of women's issues or women's experience? And we certainly don't want crossdressers or drag queens: we're not interested in representing the political concerns of men in dresses. And intersexuals who live as women? Oh, please.

An interesting contradiction rears its ugly head at this point. Although we began with the best of intentions—forming a movement to liberate women—it seems that our founding gesture is to decide who can call herself one, and then barricade the gates to prevent the barbarians from invading. Is a liberatory struggle about keeping out the "wrong people," especially those who feel they ought to be in?

If so, then regardless of who is judged a woman, an even more troubling question arises: who gets to decide? Some of us must have already been legitimized as women in order to make this determination to begin with, authorizing us to judge the rest. In so doing, we're not just keeping the riffraff out; we're creating a hierarchy where "real women" are separated from the rest of the group.

One solution, of course, is to get out of the judgment business entirely and return to plumbing: if you've got the right kind of body, you're a woman. Even momentarily putting aside the issue of intersexual women, doesn't reliance on "equipment" bring us back to a definition of *woman* in which biology becomes destiny? Doesn't it, in fact, return us to the classic oppressive construction of *woman* which defines her strictly by reproductive organs and function? Will we replace consciousness raising with crotch checks, complete with the edifying spectacle of us squatting and pointedly inspecting each other's genitals like a band of lower primates?

Worst of all, we started out wanting to liberate women. We wanted to represent their political interests and, in so doing, open up whole new horizons for them. Yet our first act has been to fence off all the things they cannot do and still be considered women. Our message is no longer, *You are free to become whatever your talent and heart allow,* but rather, *You are free to become whatever your*

talent and heart allow as long as it's not too masculine and you con-
tinue to look and act like a woman. And it appears that the woman
you will look and act like is based on the traditional, limiting,
heterosexual-based model we had hoped to chuck for good.

Instead of freeing women, we have moved to foreclose op-
tions and choices. This has the paradoxical effect of creating a liberation movement whose inaugural success is fixing and stabilizing the identity of *woman* even more firmly than before. Surely this
isn't what we intended.

BRING ON THE SIEVE

Perhaps you are thinking, "Isn't this all a philosophical sidebar?
Hasn't feminism done a good job of devoting itself to women's issues?"

To answer this, let me return to my earlier discussion about
the problems of a gay rights movement based solely on sexual orientation. While the idea of such a movement sounds straightforward enough, in application it functions like a sieve, filtering out
any issue not purely focused on sexual orientation. Left untouched
is any problem which is about "sexual orientation AND." So we're
not going to deal with queers of color, because that's sexual orientation AND race. We're not going to deal with the issues of work-
ing-class queers or queers on welfare, because that's about gay AND
class. And we're not going to deal with the concerns of lesbians,
because that's about gay AND gender.

Pretty soon, the only people we represent are those fortunate
enough to possess the luxury of a simple and uncomplicated oppression. That is, their race, class, and gender are "normal," and so
go unmarked and unoppressed. This is why the gay rights and feminist movements have done an exemplary job of representing the
needs and concerns of white, eurocentric, middle-class Americans,
but not much of anyone else.

It is turning out to be a pretty pale and bland liberation
struggle we're waging. To those at "the bottom," on the lower rungs
of the oppression ladder, the new boss looks an awful lot like the

old one. People with the greatest needs remain unrepresented and unaddressed. This is why Third World feminists at the Beijing International Women's Conference bitterly complained about the Americans' obsession with birth control, abortion rights, and sex education, while they needed to discuss male property ownership, polygamy, and female genital multilation—issues more immediately addressing their oppression.

Some theorists have tried to preserve the foundation of a politics based on identity by moving the criteria for identification from *what you are* to *what you've experienced*. A feminist movement would then represent all people who've had "women's experience." The question not asked is, is there really some universal core to women's experience transcending culture, race, history, and ethnicity? Or is this newer configuration just the umpteenth appearance of that now-familiar Western conceit that anticipates a monolithic identity and then erects its own eurocentric, heterosexual, white experience as the litmus test?

Is women's experience about raising two-point-three children in the burbs with a working husband and two cars in the garage? Is it about an urban, single, highly educated young woman on the career fast track? Or is it about polygamy, having to wear the veil, and being unable to legally drive a car or appear in public without male chaperones? If you're an HIV-positive dyke in Cuba, does that make AIDS central to the women's movement?

FOUCAULT & FRIEDAN? I THINK IT'S A LAW FIRM DOWN THE HALL

How do all these problems come about? We need to return to Foucault's observation that cultural power does not just restrain and oppress various identities, it also produces them. For instance, culture not only oppresses women, it also creates the identity of *woman*. The same goes for the identity of *homosexual, transgender,* and so on. As long as we do not pay attention to this dual nature of power, we'll continue to overlook the oppressive side effects of our own production of identity.

By basing the movement on the category *women,* we prevent ourselves from historically examining how the category came about. We assumed its existence rather than asking whose interests it serves to confine us within a binary of bodies that makes patriarchy possible to begin with.

JUST LET ME PRODUCE YOU

These are important questions because, in posing them, we gain insight into how the production of any identity inevitably creates winners and losers, those who are prelegitimized and those who are second class and "allowed" in after the fact. Until we ask these questions, we'll continue to trip over the effects of our own production of identities.

Even worse, if we *don't* ask them, we unwittingly allow the patriarchy to set the terms of our struggle. Binary sexes will remain intact and unchallenged. All that's then left for our movement to do is wrangle over the available political turf. Judith Butler talks about power's uncanny ability to generate only those rebellions that are bound to fail. When she was asked to write a piece for a gay and lesbian studies book, she replied that she could not write "as a lesbian" when the category announced a set of terms she proposed to contest."[1]

What is left to organize around if we don't use identities? While postmodernism has been largely unable and unwilling to apply itself to the nitty-gritty of social change, you and I don't have that luxury. We have a movement against gender oppression to mount.

What Butler suggests is that we allow identity to float free, that we stop barricading the gates of gender and encourage everyone to define themselves as they wish, even change their identity or invent new ones. Instead of merely tolerating this gender fluidity as a necessary evil, we accept the inherent instability of all identities and make it work for us. As new identities enter from the "outside," e.g., stone butches, trans folks, drag people, and passing women, the category expands. The boundaries blur, shift, and open. Some women become indistinguishable from men. Some women become more distinguishable from women. Some fall off that specious male–female spectrum entirely, becoming totally new genders we haven't yet named. Possibilities which our original feminism could not have foreseen or anticipated are created. Fluidity is transformed into a key feminist goal and an important liberatory tactic.

Our movement shifts its foundations from identity to one of functions of oppression. Coalitions form around particular issues, and then dissolve. Identity becomes the result of contesting those oppressions, rather than a precondition for involvement. In other words, identity becomes an effect of political activism instead of a cause. It is temporary and fluid, rather than fixed.

In practice, this means that if you identify as gender oppressed, or are interested in these issues, you're welcome in the Transexual Menace. You don't have to be a transperson, much less be judged one, in order to work within the Menace. Or, returning to the example which opened this chapter, if you're opposed to rape, you fight all rape and sexual violence, regardless of what genitals or bodies are involved. The same goes for employment discrimination. You fight it regardless of whether it's due to race, class, sexual orientation, abledness, or gender expression.

Groups as varied as the Christian Coalition and the Democratic Party have organized around issue clusters, such as abortion, welfare, and school prayer, but that's as far as it's gone.

I like to believe that if women, transpeople, or queers have learned anything from millennia of oppression, it's the experience of outsiderdom, and how the suppression of difference can kill hearts, minds, and lives. So far, unfortunately, each of these groups has waged an increasingly narrow struggle for the few at the expense of the many. Oppression, painful as it is, is also a question posed by life to each of us: will your heart grow larger, so it holds the universal hurt, or will it grow smaller, so that, in the end, it can contain only your own?

YOU KNOW ME AS RIKI FROM "AS THE GENDER TURNS." I'M

NOT A TRANSEXUAL, BUT I PLAY ONE IN REAL LIFE.

I have no interest in being part of a transgender or transexual movement whose sole purpose is to belly up to the Big Table and help ourselves to yet another serving of Identity Pie, leaving in our wake some other, more marginalized group to carry on its own struggle alone.

What I am interested in is the original cultural gesture to regulate and contain what your body and mine can mean, or say, or do. The point of a gender liberation movement for me is not just to rescue and acclaim those people sometimes referred to as "transgressively gendered," those specimens inevitably corraled in the Binary Zoo: the stone butches and diesel dykes, drag kings and drag queens, leatherdykes and dyke daddies, the radical fairies and fag hags, nelly queens and fruit flies, the transexuals, transgendered, crossdressers, and intersexed.

It is also about the seventeen-year-old Midwestern cheerleader whose health is destroyed by anorexia because "real women" are supposed to be preternaturally thin. It's about the forty-six-year-old Joe Six-Pack who wraps his car around a crowded school bus on the way home from the bar because "real men" are supposed to be heavy drinkers. It's about the unathletic and fat little boy who's physically attacked by his classmates every day after school. It's about the two lesbian lovers stalked and killed on the Appalachian trail in Virginia. It's about the aging body succumbing to an unnecessary hysterectomy because certain kinds of gendered bodies simply don't matter as much. And it's about the sensitive, straight young man who is repeatedly raped his first year in prison because, within that environment, he's perceived as genderqueer, genderdifferent, or simply gendervulnerable.

In short, a gender liberation movement is not just about people like Brandon Teena, Marsha Johnson, Christian Paige, Deborah Forte, Tyra Hunter, and Chanelle Pickett, all of whom died simply because of the way they expressed sexuality and gender. It's also about those who felt impelled and even empowered to kill to preserve the regimes of gender. In fact, it's about working until each and every one of us is delivered from this most pernicious, divisive, and destructive of insanities called gender-based oppression.

---

1. Judith Butler, "Imitation and Gender Insubordination" in *Social Theory: The Multicultural and Classic Readings,* edited by Charles Lement (Boulder, CO: Westview Press, 1993).

Photographs from a Movement

Mariette Pathy Allen

Camp Trans at Michigan Womyn's Music Festival
Hart, Michigan
August 1994

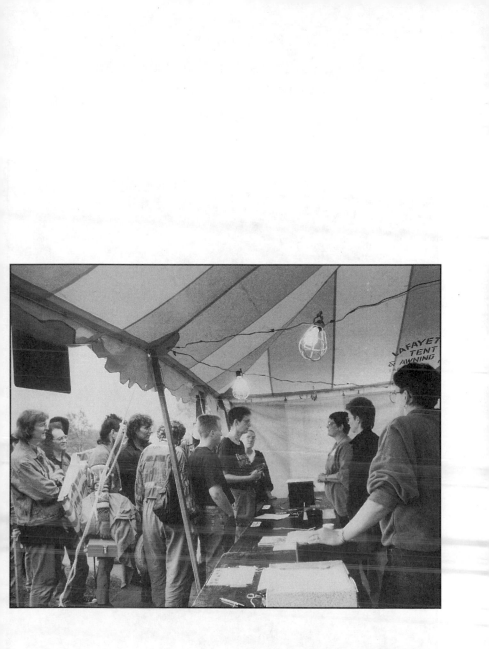

Brandon Teena Murder Trial Vigil
Falls City, Nebraska
May 1995

FIRST NATIONAL GENDER LOBBY DAY
Washington, DC
October 1995

Tyra Hunter Demonstration
Washington, DC
October 1995

SEAN O'NEILL SENTENCING
Colorado Springs, Colorado
February 1996

CHRISTIAN PAIGE VIGIL
Chicago, Illinois
May 1996

Deborah Forte Murder Trial
Cambridge, Massachusetts
September 1996

MATT STICKNEY RALLY
Burlington, Vermont
October 1996

American Psychiatric Association Meeting
Chicago, Illinois
October 1996

Chanelle Pickett Memorial Service
Cambridge, Massachusetts
December 1996

THE MENACE
IN MICHIGAN

LAST NIGHT'S RAIN IS GONE, and the afternoon sun is burning off the haze. We crossed a red clay county road separating our tents from the wood posts, wire fences, and candy-colored tents of the Michigan Womyn's Music Festival. There are six of us, gender outlaws all, queued up like so many tenpins before the smiling woman in the ticket booth. The Michigan Womyn's Music Festival is about to meet the Transexual Menace.

This rather outlandish moment had its genesis in the summer of 1991. A transexual woman, Nancy Jean Burkholder, was accosted by security guards near this very gate. The festival producers—Barbara ("Boo") Price and Lisa Vogel—had articulated a policy of "womyn-born womyn only." The security guards interpreted this to exclude transexual women and had Nancy evicted.

It's unlikely the participants in that anonymous late-night drama anticipated the chain reaction it would ignite. Within days, women across the country were talking about the eviction. Author and activist Gayle Rubin called it the "cause célèbre" of the '91 fes-

First appeared in the August 1994 issue of the *Village Voice*.

tival. As Rubin writes, "After decades of feminist insistence that women are 'made, not born,' after fighting to establish that 'anatomy is not destiny,' it is astounding that ostensibly progressive events can get away with discriminatory policies based so blatantly on recycled biological determinism."[1]

The complexities of lesbian politics have, in fact, always made the Borgias look like Ozzie and Harriet. And lesbian transphobia was hardly unique to Michigan. As early as 1972, a transexual woman was forced out of the prototype lesbian organization, Daughters of Bilitis, and as recently as 1991 the National Lesbian Conference in Atlanta banned "nongenetic women." But the festival is one of the country's oldest and most visible gatherings of lesbians, with seven or eight thousand attendees each year. For many transexuals, as well as for the larger world, it is a unique symbol of lesbian culture. More importantly, the festival is closely identified with radical lesbian separatists, feminists who embrace Mary Daly's and Janice Raymond's theory that transexual women are merely (I am not making this up) surgically altered men created by patriarchal doctors to invade women's space. For these reasons, the decision to admit "womyn-born womyn only" carried a special sting.

There have always been lesbians opposed to women appointing themselves "gender police," judging who can call themselves female and deciding which queer identities are deemed acceptable. "Despite theoretically embracing diversity," notes Rubin, "contemporary lesbian culture has a deep streak of xenophobia [responding with] hysteria, bigotry, and a desire to stamp out the offending messy realities. A 'country club syndrome' sometimes prevails in which the lesbian community is treated as an exclusive enclave from which the riffraff must be systematically expunged."[2]

Lesbians in early feminist consciousness-raising groups were told they weren't "real women"; butch-femme and S/M lesbians have been attacked for invading women's space with their oppressive, partriarchal influence. The result has been an ongoing struggle within the lesbian-feminist world against the politics of exclusion. In this spirit, the posse accompanying six gender queers into the festival's bucolic vortex in 1994 included '60s stone butch Leslie

Feinberg; '70s feminist Minnie Bruce Pratt; S/M sex outlaws from the '80s; and the '90s answer to Queer Nation, the Lesbian Avengers. What earthly power could stand against such a formidable and unholy alliance?

I could trace my own presence in Michigan back to 1978, when I began divesting the male trappings forced on me from birth, transitioning into someone nontransexuals could recognize as female. In the process, my female lover and I metamorphosed from another nice, straight couple to a couple of militant *ho-mo-seck-choo-alls* walking arm-in-arm in broad daylight down the mainstreets of Cleveland Heights, Ohio.

How is a transexual woman a lesbian? I can no more explain it than breathing, no more describe it than a smell. How is anyone a lesbian, except that she identifies as a woman and is attracted to women? Even before surgery made such things possible, desire had long since etched my dreams with soft butches and strong arms, their taxing presence inside me. In all this I was not alone, for of twelve transexual women in Camp Trans, eleven were lesbian-identified.

So I knew the name for what I was, and I knew I belonged with other lesbians. But the women's community greeted us less like prodigal sisters returned to the fold than like the unchanged kitty litter. Following a decade of fruitless efforts to claim my place in the lesbian movement, and sick of being harassed at parties, in bars, and in groups, I left for good. What was the point of tossing back brewskies with my oppressors, or fighting for a liberation that excluded the likes of me?

During the years of my premature retirement, transexuals began finding their own voices. A transexual woman today is much more likely to claim her right to define herself as female whether or not she has had surgery or is perceived as adequately feminine. Along with this newfound pride came outrage at our relentless oppression. Activist organizations with names like Transgender Nation and the Transexual Menace have sprung up across the country. We've zapped the Gay Games, Stonewall 25, various startled city councils, and, I blush to add, the *Village Voice*. News of Nancy's expulsion from Michigan reached my ears like a gunshot across the water. I looked at the last sixteen years of my life and considered my interminable struggles on the fringe of the lesbian community. Then I put on sensible shoes and headed for the fray. This bitch was back.

I joined them in 1993, after Nancy and three transexual friends had again attempted to attend the festival. Security again had asked them to leave, maintaining that radical separatists were threatening violence, and that their safety on the land could not be guaranteed. When S/M women stepped forward to ensure their safety, Security asserted the producers' "womyn- born womyn only" policy and insisted the transexuals leave. The four women did, but we refused to pack up and go home. Instead we set up camp directly across from the main gate and lobbied our case with anyone who would listen. Camp Trans was born, and in four days over two hundred festigoers stopped by to offer support, food, and water—and attend two impromptu workshops.

Camp Trans was about to become a staple of the Michigan festival, with or without official sanction.

In June of this year, a fundraiser was held in New York. For the first time a transexual event drew mainstream gay organizations, from the Lesbian Avengers to the Gay and Lesbian Alliance Against Defamation, along with mainstream queer activists like Ann Northrop, Minnie Bruce Pratt, and Amber Hollibaugh. If there is such a thing as a queer *Weltanschauung,* it was definitely moving in our direction.

Over five thousand dollars was pledged to send a bunch of gendertrash rejects to the Michigan woods. Plans were laid to fly nationally recognized queer activists from around the country for twenty-five workshops between August 10 and 14, when attendance at the festival would peak. Two thousand schedules were printed and distributed as part of our plan to draw as many women as possible to Camp Trans ("for humyn-born humyns").

So now it is Saturday afternoon and our workshops, including the first annual Mary Daly Memorial Volleyball Game: Surgically-Altered She-Male Scum vs. the World, have drawn over four hundred festigoers. One is Hillary Smith, a Lesbian Avenger from Portland, Oregon, and she, bless her subversive little heart, has recognized my Transexual Menace T-shirt. "Didn't I see you at an Avengers' meeting in Manhattan? Why don't you come to the national meeting inside?"

"Sure," I flip back, "why don't you just send me some escorts?"

"How many?" she replies, not missing a beat.

We have checked with Festival Security about this and have been told that Boo and Lisa's "womyn-born womyn only" policy stands. Unlike past years, however, each of us must interpret it for ourselves. And that is how the six of us—three pre-operative transexuals, two post-operative, one intersexed individual—happen to be here. I suspect our lives and identities are far more complex than any policy could possibly anticipate. I also suspect our grinning, excited escorts are enjoying this more than ducks in a rainstorm.

I love these strong women, but suddenly the idea that we need protection feels surreal and sad. There are sounds of nervous laughter, bad jokes, and a lot of affection going down the forty-person chain. I am wide-eyed; I have wanted to go to Michigan since 1978, and I am seeing it for the first time. Mostly it is just acres and acres of forest, tents, campsites, and women looking up with reactions as varied as they are: astonishment, confusion, laughter, applause, raised fists, smiles, angry glares, indifference.

After what seems like forever, we head up a short rise to the Avengers' meeting area. This is the first time a mainstream, national lesbian group has supported transexual women, and the scattered applause, growing to a real ovation as we come into full view, is an incredible rush. I have never seen so many young, hip dykes with good hair and straight teeth in one place, and they are all, for gosh sakes, clapping for *us*.

Afterward, fearing an angry confrontation for which we will undoubtedly be blamed, there is general consensus that, having done what we came for, we ought to just declare victory and get the hell out of Dodge. I prefer Hillary's suggestion: go to the kitchen area, sit down, and eat as if we're normal people and belong there, which, damn it, we do. We compromise: march back out, crossing the packed kitchen area at dinnertime.

Coming around a bend, I see an opening about the size of a football field with, I don't know, eight hundred, a thousand, who knows how many women in it. For a moment, it looks like the entire lesbian nation is spread out, eating, carrying food, leading children, or serving dinner. One woman, dressed entirely in studded chains and leather and sporting an enormous black strap-on, is cavorting along our path. She is going wild as we approach, and I stride up, grasping her dildo firmly, and ask, "Excuse me, can we talk?" I see women all over turning now to stare at us and, my palms suddenly moist, I breathe sotto voce, "We are going to fucking die."

You think people's mouths only drop open in cartoons or sitcoms, but I assure you their jaws actually do go slack in real life. As we're walking, festigoers see us, momentarily freeze, then just as abruptly spring back to life, trying to grok who and what we are. Applause breaks out, the odd raised fist, a few waves, and finally lots and lots of smiles. Almost without exception, these women support our cause. By now we are all beaming as well; I myself am grinning like an idiot at anyone within range. I am suddenly aware, clearly and precisely, that lesbian politics is changing—fundamentally, irrevocably, right before my eyes.

How do I feel? Being transexual is like a tax: you pay it to get a job, rent an apartment, find a lover, just exist. Phrases like *womyn-born womyn only, biological women only, genetic women only,* or whatever exclusionary formula is in vogue, cut deeply. With each hurt I hear anew Alice Walker's admonition never to be the only one in the room, and recall that as a transexual woman, I am usually the only one in the room. But not today. Today I have sisters: protecting me, standing beside me, honoring my presence. Mostly just being here feels like coming home.

---

1. Gayle Rubin, "Of Catamites and Kings" in *The Persistent Desire: A Femme-Butch Reader* (Boston: Alyson, 1993), p. 466.

2. Ibid.

Our Cunts Are
Not the Same

From time to time I do a workshop I first performed at Camp Trans, "Our Cunts Are Not the Same: Transexual Sexuality and Sex-Change Surgery." I gratefully credit the idea to Annie Sprinkle, from whom I unblushingly stole it. Annie does a hands-on fist-fucking segment, as well as an "examine my cervix" portion, in her performance art. She was kind enough to share some of her tips with me on how to carry such a thing off.

The first half is comfortingly didactic. I discuss the various techniques and technologies of surgery. I describe what it feels like. I use lots of medical terms. Everyone seems at ease. They ask intelligent, sensitive questions. I try to give intelligent, sensitive answers.

Then I tell them we are moving from the theoretical to the experiential. This portion I lovingly refer to as the Show 'n' Tell, Touch 'n' Feel, or sometimes, Scratch 'n' Sniff.

Drop Your Drawers: It's Going to Be a Bumpy Ride

I drop my drawers. Since, unlike Annie, I am not an artiste and I don't get paid for this, everyone who wants to stay drops her drawers as well. At Camp Trans, we had about two dozen people. We thought maybe three or four might stick around. Since it was my first time, that was fine with me. It was all I felt I could handle.

We were wrong. You could have gone deaf from the sound of jeans hitting the deck. To my horror, every single woman stayed, and all were looking expectantly, trustingly at me.

At the National Women's Music Festival, held annually in Bloomington, Indiana, we had the opposite reaction. Several people were trampled in the rush for the door. Luckily, I got to administer mouth-to-mouth. No matter. Again about two dozen intrepid souls were left when the dust cleared, and Science continued its relentless march onward. Neither snow, nor rain, nor dark of night can stop me from getting felt up by twenty women.

For the Scratch 'n' Sniff, everyone pulls on latex gloves (safe sex only) and gets to feel a real live transcunt. It's no big deal for me; I do it all the time. But for them it's a different matter.

Several interesting things occur, the least of which is that people fall apart. For many women, this is a gut-wrenching experience. It's one thing to talk about sex-change surgery, argue about whether I'm a real woman and all that jazz. It's another entirely to find your hand buried to the knuckles inside the warm, breathing body of another person—to feel the heat of my body, the smooth skin of my vagina, to watch my hips move if you hit the right place.

This matter with my hips has occasionally gotten, so to speak, out of hand. I sometimes forget I am among lesbians. It usually begins as an experiment. One woman hits that certain spot, my hips turn, and before you can say, "read my lips," all of them are trying it. Pretty soon, I feel more like the losing end of lesbian target practice than a show 'n' tell exhibit. Then some girl gets the smart idea of seeing if she can make me moan a little. Then someone tries to make me moan a lot. It's about this point that I have to call a halt to the proceedings: after all, we're scientists here, not sluts.

At Bloomington, the lover of one participant accused her partner of infidelity because she had fucked me. Explanations that this was Science, that it was nonsexual, even that I wasn't really another female, were to no avail.

Another participant discovered her friends from home were so grossed out that she had touched a transexual cunt, "a man's cunt!" (I don't make 'em up, folks), that they stopped speaking to her. She related all this to me through tears, because these were people she had come to the festival with and had known since childhood. She was astonished to discover how transphobic they were toward me, and correspondingly quick to turn on her, as if I were contagious. What was even stranger was that her outraged friends were so deliciously and completely butch, they made me feel like I was an extra in petticoats straight out of *Gone with the Wind*.

A nonparticipant, who had read of the workshop in the festival's schedule of events, was so offended by the idea that she wrote a scathing letter to the board. It was caustic and rich in feminist invective, and probably would have been effective except that the board member to whom it was addressed had not only had her own hand in me up to the wrist (ouch!), but had also taken it upon herself to essay an unscheduled excursion up my asshole as well, something I was quickly and loudly constrained to point out was not on our afternoon's trip-tik adventure.

BUT WHAT A DEEP PENIS YOU HAVE, GRANDMA!

Another interesting thing happens when I ask all participants, in the strongest terms possible, to refer to the area in question as my penis. I remind them that many trans vaginas are actually constructed by inverting the penis, so I would prefer that they refer to mine by its original name.

It's not important that that is not the particular surgery I had. The point is, they are unable to follow my instructions. Nearly all the participants do three things while exploring my penis: first, they exclaim about the wonders of modern surgery; second, they invariably refer to it as a cunt; and third, they declaim about how it's just like theirs.

I have come to understand that some very active visual and semiotic construction is going on. It's simply impossible, it seems, for festival participants to relate to my genitals as other than a cunt.

It is true that we tend to organize our visual field into familiar signs, especially something as fundamental and visceral as genitals. What would someone say to make sense of and eroticize my crotch: "Oh, I just love Riki's cock and I'd love to stick my tongue deep down inside it?" This is just not an erotically intelligible statement. The only way to comprehend my genitals is through reinscribing them as a cunt. Of course, this is exactly what many transwomen want. I have no moral or religious objections to it either.

FRANKLY MY DEAR, I DON'T GIVE A DAMN

But what of Holly Boswell? Holly is a delicate Southern belle of long acquaintance. I may occasionally feel like an extra from *Gone with the Wind,* but Holly actually is one. S/he has tender features, long, wavy blonde hair, a soft Carolina accent, a delicate feminine bosom, and no interest in surgery. Holly lives as an openly trans-gendered mother of two in Asheville, North Carolina. Her comforting advice to confused citizens struggling with whether to use *Sir* or *Madam* is, "Don't give it a second thought. You don't have a pronoun yet for me." This goes over famously in the Deep South.

Now, just between you and me, I confess that for some time now I have had this killer crush on Holly's tender young flesh. We've chatted about this together, engaging in a lot of half-hearted flirting and affectionate banter when our paths have crossed at various gender conventions. What we have also discussed, and what is even more interesting for me, is the question Holly's body poses. If she ever took my banter seriously and we became involved, what would I do with her body?

JUST HAND ME THAT COLLAR ON THE NIGHTSTAND, WILL YOU?

It is not at all clear what Holly's body means to me. For starters, how I would eroticize her penis? I mean, would she mount me from behind and make me bark like the dog I am? I might enjoy this idea, but I don't think Holly would entertain it, if only because I don't think that's the way she conceives of her genitals. Would I treat it as a big clit? Or would I have to find some completely new meaning?

I don't suppose I should need any meaning at all, except that eroticism is connected in some fundamental way to what things mean: virility, softness, strength, vulnerability, and so on; this tells me that gender, that notorious difference engine, is hard at work here, defining and delimiting what things count as erotic.

For me to eroticize Holly's body, particularly her genitals, requires that I do some quick, intense reinscribing. It is obvious to me that her inscription of what her penis means does not match my own idea of what penises mean. To negotiate sex between us would therefore mean negotiating new meanings.

The idea of negotiating erotic meanings can lead to interesting situations. For example, how do we eroticize those always-absent bodies: intersexed (hermaphroditic) bodies, whose genital formations may be quite different from, or contain mixed features of, what we normally conceive of as genitals? What does a "large clit" or a "small penis," either one combined with a vaginal opening, mean? How do they challenge and subvert our understanding of eroticism?

And please do not refer me to arguments of pathology or functioning. It is manifestly the case that some intersexed bodies function well sexually, and sometimes in ways we cannot imagine. Holly described to me a wonderful intersexed adult video that I have been trying to get my grubby little hands on. It is of two people, both with penises and cunts, penetrating and being penetrated by each other, simultaneously. She said it was the most complete, moving, and beautiful merging of two human bodies she had ever witnessed.

Transbodies and transgenitals create uncertainty and anxiety among many people. Straight men are afraid that by fucking transwomen they become fags. Straight women are confused about what to do with nonoperative male transsexuals in bed. Married women are unsure of what to do with their husbands' penises peeping out at them from lace satin panties under silk dressing gowns. Gay men are confused by the appearance of "transfags," transsexual men who are gay but have not gotten or do not want a penis. Lesbians are conflicted about what it means to sleep with transwomen who "were" men, or who still have penises, or who may still have masculine characteristics. On the other hand, other lesbians are genuinely confused with their butch lovers who decide they're really transexual men, and start dressing in men's clothes, taking testosterone, growing beards, and packing dildos.

Activist (and, if personal experience is any guide, world-class sex pervert) Nancy Nangeroni has observed that all this confusion means many transpeople will spend most of their romantic lives alone. By crossing the lines of gender, you cross the lines of eroticism. You also cross the lines of aesthetics. Bodies which combine differently gendered parts and displays often appear disconcerting, disturbing, ridiculous, or simply enigmatic to others. Finding a partner under these circumstances becomes much, much harder.

Loneliness, and the inability to find partners, is one of the best-kept secrets in the transcommunity. It's something many of us carry around like a private shame, a secret wound we hide from view. This is because we are convinced the isolation only confirms our deepest fears—that we are somehow deficient. It should remind us instead, once again, that the personal is political.

The gender system, which marks many kinds of bodies as either nonerotic or erotically problematic, is at work in the most intimate spaces of our lives. We fall off the grid of erotic intelligibility which sections the body into known, recognizable parts. Transbodies are the cracks in the gender sidewalk. When we find partners, they must be willing to negotiate the ambiguity of the terrain.

ONE IMPORTED WATER AND TWO DESIGNER GENITALS TO GO, PLEASE

For years, I really hated this little spot on my body. I shared my concern in support groups and recovery meetings, sobbing and unable to hide my shame. It was a small portion of my penis. To create my clit, the doctor had transplanted the head of my penis between my newly formed lips, waited a few months, and then carved it down to look "real."

The fact that I still had this part of my penis, including a section just below my urethra which got distinctly hard when I was aroused, that my glans had actually lived between my labia for nearly three months, humiliated me. I overate because of it. I tried to ignore my body when I masturbated. Of course, it's much harder to masturbate when you're ignoring your body. But in my mind's eye, I could still see that glans, implanted like some creature from *Alien*, about to burst out of my groin and attack Sigourney Weaver.

Current practice in sex-change surgery assumes, even requires, "real-looking" genitals. Otherwise, what's the point? It also assumes, and even requires, that transpeople desire "real-looking" genitals. This is why so many doctors, while proudly showing off how "their vagina" can even fool OB/gyns, are reduced to muttering "no guarantees" and "we can't be certain" when asked about the pleasure potential of their work. It's also part of why many transwomen don't have a lot of erotic sensation after surgery. We don't ask as much about how it will feel as we do about how it will look.

This same medical obsession with looks is why so many intersexed infants survive their nonconsensual sex-change-type surgeries with little erotic sensation later in life. What are genitals if they are not either penises or cunts? We all want our groins to look just like real men's and women's, don't we, even if we must carve infants' flesh to achieve that all-important illusion?

But suppose all these assumptions are false. The longer I've lived with my little bit of penis, my clit, and my vagina, the more I've asked myself why I had them cut so much of it away. Don't get me wrong. I really like my body, but I don't want a "woman's" body. I don't imagine myself borrowing "parts" that another gender owns. I really like penetrative sex as well as using a vibrator. But couldn't I have kept just a tad more tissue and with it a little more sensation? I ask myself this with the benefit of 20/20 hindsight, since, at the time, I actually believed the purpose of the operation was to "make me a woman." Sigh.

And of course, the only surgery most doctors will perform is one from column *A* or one from column *B:* there is no intermediate ground. But as Dana Priesing notes, if Nature naturally makes intersexed people, then what could possibly be wrong with wanting to become intersexed? In fact, why not bite the bullet and admit that intersex genitals, instead of being defective versions of "the real thing," are often different, most interesting, or simply...better?

Logically, since surgery doesn't make one anything, nor does having a penis prevent one from being anything else, why can we not have designer genitals? I reasoned this before I'd heard of it in reality. I knew that transmen who undertook surgery attempted various kinds of penises, but various kinds of cunts?

Then my friend Hannah approached me about having surgery. She was interviewing surgeons, and wondered how my surgery had been done. When we finished talking, she said she wanted to keep her entire glans and as much sensitivity as possible. She later polled her lesbian friends on how they would cope sexually with her new groin. True to form, they reconstructed the available erotic categories right onto her body without a blink, quickly declaring that it would be just a nice, big clit.

Interestingly, the well-known surgeon who performed the surgery was willing to do so only under protest. He informed her it was mutilation (!?) and perversion. I am fairly confident he meant perversion here as a bad thing. Anyway, I suppose his idea was that wanting your dick sewn into a real-looking cunt was normal, but getting creative and inserting your own aesthetics into the process was not.

My Hannah stuck with it, staring back at him calmly and declaring that it was her body, her money, and this was what she wanted. Perversion or no, it was what she was going to get. He relented.

Who knows how the frontiers can be explored as we move forward? Suppose the market grows and the big design houses get directly involved. They already gladly put their logos on everything from pillowcases to cars. Why not genitals? Maybe someday you'll be able to order a Gucci (continental, comes with matching shoes and handbag), a Bill Blass (very corporate "power" genitals), a Shelby-Cobra (high-torque penis with overhead cam, kick start, and four-hundred horsepower), or, for that truly safe sex, a Volvo (roll it over and walk away without a scratch).

And so here I am, still struck by the notion of one of my best

friends serenely ordering for take-out the very same designer genitals which for nearly ten years reduced me to a quivering lump of
hot, humiliated tears. Such is the power of ideas and beliefs to wreak
vengeance in the mind.

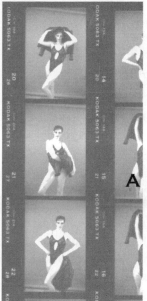

A FASCISM
OF MEANING

FLUID MEANINGS

I am sitting through that obligatory, apparently interminable nightmare of the high school curriculum: the health & science class. But today I will at last learn the secrets of those delicate blue-lined drawings I found in my sister's dresser drawer, showing young women happily inserting various kinds of cardboard tubes into obscure orifices. The drawings are surrounded by frothy, mysterious vignettes like:

> *How to Use Clampax Poontons: The clue to proper insertion is to* get hold of yourself. *If it helps, take two Valium or attend your TM session beforehand, but just make sure you are calm and relaxed; otherwise the muscles of your vaginal opening will snap shut like the valves of a scared mollusk. No need to worry. Millions of girls just like you learned to walk normally again, and you will, too!*

> *Will anybody be able to tell that I'm menstruating and*

*wearing Clampax? In addition to you, only clairvoyants,
dogs, and men will know for sure.*[1]

Yes, today we are to learn the mysteries of menstruating (*not*
Menace-trating, which involves T-shirts and picketing and is a different thing altogether).

But wait, there's more! Yes, today we have the health & science
double feature. We're going to cover ejaculation. Now, ejaculation
has been a real problem of mine, because I seem to be doing a great
deal of it lately. I have a book, *Sex for Teenagers: Frank Talk for Honest Questions*. It has this happy teen hetero couple on the cover,
holding hands, gazing brightly into each other's eyes, and somehow managing to look both uncertain and frisky simultaneously.
And yes, it covers masturbation.

It says, "Most normal teenagers find it necessary to masturbate to completion from time to time." I've read that part over about
twenty times now, consulting it as if it were the Delphic Oracle. But
what do they mean by *completion?* Is that ejaculation, or does it
mean merely stopping when you feel kind of finished? Maybe most
normal teens feel completion right before the final act. Maybe for
them just a few good strokes in the shower is enough and, unlike
certifiable perverts like me, they don't find it necessary to jerk off
until they actually (yuck!) ejaculate.

In fact, on the critical subject of masturbation, it doesn't say a
word about coming home from school, scrambling down into the
basement and across the laundry room to lock yourself in the most
distant bathroom in the house so you can add yet another hand-
kerchief, wadded together like a cement sculpture, to the growing
collection in the laundry hamper which by now, surely, your mother,
the cleaning lady, or both must have noticed. In fact, I am convinced the only reason they haven't denounced me to the Sex Police and had me carted away is that, having graciously turned down
all increases in my allowance, I'm very cheap to keep around. Moreover, because they—like most normal teens of *their* day—probably
found it necessary to masturbate to completion from time to time,
they're cutting me some slack.

But I don't know for sure, and there's no adult at hand I can readily ask. I mean, some evening over dinner, I can't chime in with, "Pass the carrots, would you, Sis? Hey, Dad, I was just wondering, did you or Mom ever masturbate to completion when you were a kid?"

I'LL SHOW YOU MY FLUIDS IF YOU SHOW ME YOURS

So I am ready, even desperate, to learn today. And lucky for me, Science seems to have pinned all this down pretty well.

It seems that menstruation entails the discharge from the body of a couple of teaspoons of lukewarm fluid. This discharge occurs about once a month for a number of years, and women's bodies lose perhaps five hundred gametes slowly over about forty years. This process is unfailingly described by both the scientific literature and the teacher in the most unambiguous terms of bodily waste, loss, weakness, and general femininity. Inevitably stressed is the loss of the cell which, if it were only properly deployed, could have led to a live human being. The boys look over at the girls, who are uniformly staring at the floor, aghast and ashamed at all the little potential human beings leaking out of their bodies, perhaps even at that moment.

We move on to ejaculation. This part is much better. It seems that ejaculation entails the discharge from the body of a couple of teaspoons of lukewarm fluid. This discharge occurs—oh, up to five times a day—for a number of years, and men's bodies lose perhaps two gazillion (the number is imprecise here) gametes each time: little potential human beings sprayed into the carpet, handkerchiefs, rolled pieces of liver, hollowed-out pumpkins, almost anything you can name. No matter, I am gratified to note that this process is unfailingly described by both the scientific literature and the teacher in the most unambiguous terms of virility, dominance, strength, potency, and general masculinity. The girls now stare over at the boys with open envy, while the boys themselves are lost in rapt contemplation of their own pubescent, potent crotches.

THE WOMAN IN THE BODY

The teenage years that follow are both hard to remember and difficult to forget. They are filled with things I do not want to recall: all the boys trying on the cocksure walk of men; the knowing laugh, the rude gesture, the practiced invective; struggling to out-butch each other in the now-serious struggles for dominance interspersed with occasional quick and violent fistfights; the running, seemingly endless commentary on intercourse in which the girl is inevitably "stacked."

The girls, for their part, do not resist this appropriation of their bodies, but instead accept it as natural. They become increasingly self-conscious of their breasts and hips, which have become a portal of vulnerability. A mere pointed gaze at these from any of us is enough to cause a tightened jaw, a quickened stride, or sometimes a flirtatious smirk. They begin to form their own complementary pecking order based largely on boy-popularity, chest size, good looks, and, of course, that indispensable quality—thinness.

All in all, everyone learns what their bodies are supposed to mean, how they are to act as they become the totally predictable things fate has in store.

For me this meant becoming all boy, all of the time. It was a time of profound loss of self because there appeared to be no alternative, so that the whole thing seemed not so much something that was being done to me as the inevitable consequence of what I actually was. My body, which had simply been my body, became a place imbued with a confusing welter of meanings I was required to gain command of and navigate through in order to survive, all of them natural and thus inescapable.

A SPECIAL APPROPRIATION

Puberty is often described as a time when adolescents experience great anxiety, mood swings, and confusion due to hormonal and bodily changes. I propose a more culturally laden, less biological source for such behaviors: once society begins to "see" our pubescent bodies as potential surfaces for eroticism and procreation, it descends upon us with all the subtlety of an iron fist.

Girls growing breasts, boys growing pubic hair and deeper voices, suddenly find we have to memorize and master an entire set of adult meanings. It is not just that things as static signs, like bodies, must mean certain things, but also that we must maintain a consonance between those meanings and our entire expressive language of possible clothing, gesture, and stance. This dressage of gender becomes a daily ritual and begins to dictate our lives and our interrelationships. Girls are brought down from the trees, boys from playing with the girls.

Adults begin to observe us—no longer to keep us from the dangers of crossing the street, but from the dangers of crossing gender rules. We, in turn, learn to observe ourselves and to police each other. Anyone who has been the subject of or witness to the taunting, ostracism and intimidation visited by teens upon a genderqueer—the special venom and unique savagery—must wonder where we learned it. No wonder is necessary: we taught ourselves.

I remember seeing Diane Stein sunbathing in a two-piece swimsuit as I shot baskets in her backyard and the sudden shaft of pain, of realization, that the lovely body she exposed to the sun was now as distant, as unobtainable for me as the planet Mars, and that a part of me was irrevocably lost. I don't know how many hours I've invested in the years since, trying to get back to whoever I was before that afternoon.

For the first time I learned shame; not for what I had or hadn't done, but for what I *was*. And for what I *knew*. The knowledge broke upon me anew each day in school. In order to survive, I was going to have to lie a great deal—to my parents, my teachers, and my friends, and not just with my words, but with my body and my actions.

It was not just the back of my father's hand that I feared, or the beatings after school, or even the general ostracism, although that would have been more than enough, but a strange feeling that something else lurked out there for genderqueers, something that was truly dangerous. Something waited for me that ate little queers raw, and at the time, I didn't know what it was. For years I chalked it up to paranoia, until I came across the phenomenon of Psychiatric Abuse of Gender-Variant Children (PAGC). These were stories of teenagers put on locked wards, subjected to involuntary therapy, and treated to round-the-clock behavior modification for being only marginally more genderqueer in their actions than I was in my heart.

Even if we do not physically violate the bodies of our children, certainly we possess them in every way: the shape and color and texture of every child's eroticism, sexuality, and gender is a cultural property. Children don't own their own bodies. Despite the fact that we tell ourselves how concerned we are about maintaining some mythical innocence to childhood sexuality, despite our national obsession with kiddy porn, it is hard to escape the conclusion that puberty is when our culture eats its young.

And if this whole process falls more heavily on transgendered and "prehomosexual" children, if—as I increasingly suspect—it is all too often accompanied not by a metaphoric incest or sexual violation but by a real and physical one, then it is only because, within this baroque system, genderqueer kids present an ideal profile for sexual predators. We are often emotionally transparent, hungry for adult attention and approval, out of touch with our own bodies, socially isolated, lacking in any sense of boundaries, confused about what is "normal," and used to keeping secrets about our bodies. If there are sharks in the water, the social thrashing of genderqueer kids is bound to attract them. Such abuse appears not as an anomaly but as a cultural norm: the means by which genderqueer kids are instructed in the limits and consequences of gender difference.

THE BODY AS A SITE OF CONSTRAINT AND AUTHORIZATION

What has become apparent is that my physical person—its perceived properties, size, weight, curvature—has been pressed into service by society as a site of *constraint* and *authorization*. Constraint, because some meanings are disallowed me by my own flesh. Authorization, because having certain characteristics authorizes me—obliges me—to feel certain things, to have a particular sense of myself. In fact, I suspect that the issue is not so much freeing my "self" as uncovering the ways in which this particular self is a product of culture—again, an historical item, as much as the clothes I wear or the books I read. Just like them, it was created, distributed, and promoted in responses to highly specific, if diffuse, cultural needs.

I am reminded of a friend I spoke with whom I addressed as a woman. She'd been considering surgery between bouts of cross-dressing and deep depression. She responded that she could not ever possibly be a woman, since she had a big belly, hairy arms, and a penis. I responded that that was exactly the kind of woman I liked. She broke down in tears.

If human beings were forced to march from one person to another, announcing things about themselves that made them feel dreadful, or made to carry signs inscribed with the painful words, we would instantly recognize this as a terrible assault. But what about a system which uses the body itself as a text to announce certain things? What about the large-breasted woman, for example, who feels that whenever she enters a room, her body is forced to say, "I am sexually provocative and sensuous?" If you happen to wear a 44-D cup, you are going to have to constantly work uphill professionally against what your breasts are perceived to be saying to the world.

The use of bodies to constrain or authorize various meanings and feelings doesn't affect only transpeople. Why is it that it is okay in this society to be "fat and lazy," or "fat and jolly," but not "fat and sexy"? Why is it that fat people often have tremendous difficulty seeing themselves as sexy, or, if they do, are not allowed to display that meaning? If people perceive you as fat, try walking out the door in New York City in a lowcut blouse, short skirt, and high heels and see if you can make it to the subway without being humiliated.

In my case, I was constrained from feeling things about my body and obliged to feel others. I was denied access to the broad range of nonverbal language with which we express our sense of self: in posture, gesture, clothing, adornment, and inflection. This, in turn, helped constrain what I actually felt, for, as anyone knows, it is a difficult maneuver to feel something and simultaneously refrain from expressing it nonverbally. Visibility can be a trap.

To avoid displaying any of the "inappropriate" and prohibited signs about myself, I policed myself from feeling them, lest I give myself away with a gesture, a stance, or anything that would allow others to smell that *something* about me was not right, that would single me out and make me a target for social retribution. Most times I succeeded; sometimes, I failed. At certain junctures I didn't need to police myself; there didn't seem to be any choice. I acted "masculine" in those circumstances not because I was forced to, but because that seemed, in some inexpressible way, to be what I was, and, since there was pretty much universal agreement about it, acting otherwise was unthinkable.

In general, I got better and better at hiding my feelings deeper and farther away, until they were completely hidden, even from me. A good bit of my life is now given over to a kind of introspective archaeology, where I try to unearth and piece together parts of myself lost to antiquity. Each discovery, like the surfacing of a hidden incident of childhood abuse or violation, brings with it fresh pain and fresh tears and still, even at my age, a surprisingly robust and often irrational sense of fear.

A FASCISM OF MEANING

All of which is pretty ridiculous, since meanings do not cling to bodies like some kind of glutinous vapor or semiotic paste. On the contrary, every meaning attaching to our bodies was put there by someone, long ago. Every gendered scar on my psyche has distinctly nontransexual fingerprints, and they show up with the lightest dusting and in the poorest light.

These are crimes, but they are small, silent, daily crimes, and the ensuing screams are swallowed in a vacuum. They are not crimes of passion but crimes of meaning, the imposition of a kind of "fascism of meaning" which robs us of our bodies at an early age and bids us recognize ourselves, and be perpetually recognized, in very specific ways. In effect, we require dominance/power displays in our men, and submission/vulnerability displays in our women. And to speed them in fulfilling this universal cultural requirement, we construct male bodies as meaning dominance and power, and female bodies as meaning submission and vulnerability. It is as coercive and unconsenting as being named, and infinitely more indelible.

For some people this pressure is like a vise, and it squeezes them until nothing is left. I have observed people walk into trans-support groups who had been left practically speechless, watched them sit through entire meetings in mute silence. I am reminded of a close herm-friend of mine, a particularly brilliant, charming, and resourceful person who, when I inquired after her obvious difficulty navigating even the most basic social situations, replied, "Well, you know, I lived the first twenty years of my life in a paper bag."

In the midst of this punishing system, I have also seen the most astonishing resilience and dignity on faces, a buoyancy and survivorship transcending circumstance. I suspect this is because at heart we, in all our messy complexity, are much more stubborn and rude and resourceful than the political system which seeks to invest us with shame.

THE SEARCH FOR RESONANCE

To navigate in a society of human beings, to *think oneself* at all, one must have a self: a specific organization of flesh, soul, and meaning, a mental sign which stands for "this person" having certain properties and characteristics.

Monique Wittig has observed that "...the first, the permanent, and the final social contract is language."[2] Our bodies—as signs in that language—are the first and most permanent element of that linguistic contract, and in order to participate in the social space of language, we agree to be our "selves" as we are seen by others, that is, our particular physical selves—fat or thin, black or white, young or old. The most basic part of that linguistic contract to which our bodies are apprenticed is to be sexed, and being sexed in this context does not mean agreeing to mouth the words "I am female," to answer to the name, or to mark the box next to *Male* with an *X*. It means agreeing to feel and look and act your sex, to participate in society as a meaningful member within the matrix of expectations that go along with your sex.

If it is true that at this point in human development we must have a "self," perhaps the single most profound and private thing we can create on our journey through this life is our sense of who and what we are. This is not a problem for most of us. We inherit meanings for ourselves which are more or less acceptable.

For others, the self which resonates within us is entirely at odds with what culture works to inscribe on our flesh. And this inaugurates a lifelong battle. To be so taxed with a cultural body whose meanings not only fail to resonate, but which actively militate against our deepest sense of what is meaningful, consequential, and true at every turn, to have this experience is to feel a unique kind of discomfort and pain. It affords little respite. For it is not just there in the shower, in dating situations, before strangers on the street, when applying for a job, undressing, in the act of making love, and in the eyes of family and friends, but it is also in our heads whenever we think about what constitutes "me."

When I refused to acquiesce, when I fought back, persisting in my insubordination, I was obliged to occupy that gender gulag, that spare, oblique wasteland known as *transgender*. And please don't tell me we're going to resuscitate the term so that I can inhabit it with comfort and newfound pride. I am not interested in taking up residence in forced housing no matter how nicely it's dressed up for the occasion. I'm also not interested in the "freedom" to self-identify within a host of readymade, off-the-rack social constructs whose boundaries and requirements are completely removed from my determination.

Nor am I interested in those supposedly more sophisticated solutions seeking to locate my identity as falling somewhere along a marvelous "spectrum of gender," one inevitably anchored and dominated by identities which aren't my own. I have too often been obliged to speak my name in and through the political category of *transgender,* because, as I was told, people like me transgressed gender, when it is manifestly the case that it is gender which has transgressed all over me.

What I *am* interested in is access to distinctly different ways of organizing my self, which do not first require that I have such and such a kind of body or sexuality in order to be heard, which do not require of me that I have any specific identity at all in order to participate.

---

1. Peg Bracken, "Money" in *Titters*, edited by Deane Stillman (New York: Collier Books, 1976), p. 130.

2. Monique Wittig, *The Straight Mind and Other Essays* (Boston: Beacon Press, 1992), p. 34.

CLICK.
HELLO?

CLICK. Hello?

Yes. Hello, I'm a transexual woman and I—
CLICK.
Hello? Hello?

Yes. Hello, I'm interested in changing the sex on my driver's—
CLICK.
Hello? Hello?

Yes. Hi. I'm just your normal female woman and I notice they've made a mistake on my driver's license, ha-ha, and put me down, ha-ha, wait till you get this, as a man. Can you tell me how I can get this changed? What?...I'll have to bring my birth certificate down with my correct sex on it so you can verify it? Okay.
CLICK.

Hello? County Records Office? I'm a transexual and I—

CLICK.
Hello? Hello?

Yes? County Records Office? I'm trying to get my driver's license corrected. You see, it lists me as a man and they told me that to get it changed I have to get a copy of my birth certificate and—
CLICK.
Hello? Hello?

County Records? Yes. I'm just your average woman here in the county, and yesterday, just looking through some old papers, I noticed a couple errors on my birth certificate and I was just kind of wondering, you know, woman-to-woman here, how I could get them corrected...uh-huh...submit a doctor's statement contemporaneous with my birth from the attending physician or else a notarized statement from my current personal physician and a second notarized statement from a physician here in the county of origin. Thank you.
CLICK.

Yes. Doctor's office? I'd like to speak with—
Please hold, Sir.
CLACK...
...
...
...
...
...
CLICK.

Hello, doctor's office? Yes, I just called. Please don't put me on—
Can you hold please, Sir?
CLACK...
...
...

CLICK.

Yes. I've been put on hold twice. Can I please talk to Dr. Sprocket?

I'm connecting you now, Sir.

Doctor Sprocket? This is Riki Anne Wilchins. Right. I know you've only seen me a couple of times but now that I've started hormones and everything I'm having trouble finding work as a woman and I need to change—

CLONCK.

Hello? Hello?

Yes. Doctor? Yes, well we were cut off. As I was saying, I'm trying to change my driver's license so I can get a job but they want my birth certificate and that's still male so I have to get that changed and to do that I'll need a statement from you that—no, I can't take time off from work to come in to see you.... Well, first I can't because I have no job to take time from and second because I can't afford another $150 visit—no, I'm not trying to be difficult.... Yes, I know surgeons are very busy and they save lives and all but...look, if you could please just see your way clear to—

CLICK.

Hello? Hello?

Doctor? Doctor Sprocket? Yes. I'm sorry I got angry, Doctor. Look, is there any way you could sign a statement that I'm female so I can get my paperwork done and get a job?... I know you can't be certain yet but how many men want to take estrogen and grow bosoms?... Oh, really? I had no idea.... Yes, I know I still sleep with women and that's not very normal for a transexual.... No, I haven't looked very feminine when I've come for my appointments. Have you ever tried walking around the city in a push-up bra, pantyhose, three-inch heels, and— Oh, really? I had no idea. Then you know what I— No, I wasn't aware you wear women's panties under your smock when you operate, but I can certainly sympathize with— What? You want me to see what?... Who?... Is there any way we could avoid this?... Okay. Okay, yes. I'm sure you're looking out for my interests. Good-bye.

CLICK.

Hello? Hello? Dr. Farvis? Dr. Francis Farvis? Yes. This is Riki Anne Wilchins. Yes. That's right...from Dr. Sprocket. Yes, Thursday is fine...afternoon is fine. How much? You said how much?? Is that absolutely necessary?... Okay, okay. Yes, I want to get my paperwork done... Yes, I'll be there at four o'clock sharp.... No, believe me, Doctor, it won't be any trouble getting off work.... No, I haven't been in therapy before.... Yes, I'll try to come properly dressed. Speaking of which, did you know that Dr. Sprocket— No, never mind, just thinking out loud.... Yes, I know thinking out loud could be a sign of— Well, of course I sound a little agitated and defensive, Doctor. Now let me ask you a question: Do you have any idea at all how frustrating it can be going through all this stuff and getting a sex-change operation and— Oh really? I had no idea. Yes...yes...okay, I'll see you Thursday. Good-bye, Doctor.

CLICK.

Hello? City Court? Yes, I'm a transexual woman and I need to get my name changed and—

CLICK.

Hello? Hello?

IMAGINARY BODIES,
IMAGINING MINDS

You make me feel like a natural woman.

Aretha Franklin (Carole King) song

Damn it, when I put on a skirt and heels it makes me feel like a woman and, I hate to admit it, but sometimes I like that.

Androgynous lesbian-feminist in women's rap group

All I ever wanted was to feel like a man.

Transexual man

I lusted, I pined, to look like, act like, and be accepted as a nontransexual woman. I believed in my heart that there was a marble altar in a hidden temple somewhere, surrounded by flickering candles and hooded acolytes, with the word FEMALE indelibly inscribed upon it. Only nontransexual women could attend it, only nontransexual women knew where it was, and only nontransexual women selected who was or wasn't allowed in. And I was not. At best, I might be allowed to approach, the precise distance depending upon from what quarter the winds of political correctness blew at that moment.

Author's unpublished manuscript

Nothing in man—not even his body—is sufficiently stable to serve as the basis for self-recognition or for understanding other men.

Michel Foucault[1]

Contemplating that mythical altar, how is it possible for me to want to feel "like a woman" in the same way as my lesbian-feminist friend who occasionally dons heels and a skirt? Since we both want to feel that way, how is it possible for us *not* to? How do we construct and recognize a particular state as feeling "like a woman," a state that, on the one hand, we are both able to experience, yet on the other, subsequently reflect upon and realize it is not what we customarily feel?

We can well ask, in fact, given that bodies can mean so many things, and that multiple internal experiences exist, how is it possible for us to feel "like" anything at all? How are certain feelings centered, focused, and solidified into a recognizable form? Finally, how is it possible that we can identify features of our bodies as internal experiential states, like feeling ugly, or fat, or tall, or like a woman? While one can *be* any of these things, what can it mean to *feel* them as well?

In short, how is the knowledge of one's body being a social identity (woman/man), or being read as having a particular physical property (tall/feminine/fat), converted and congealed into a specific, internal feeling, an identifiable subjective experience?

These questions are generally overlooked in feminist literature because the answers usually lead to a Jamesian kind of introspection where you examine your own subjective states and try to figure out what is going on. It is a process that is messy, easy to critique, and much more challenging than talking in general theoretical terms. Transpeople, however, as well as others trapped in unpleasant and painful bodily meanings, do not have the luxury of ignoring this inquiry. For the identification of being trans, if it is about anything, is about the private experience of profoundly important and complex subjective states. This is a mountain we cannot go around or over. Only through.

PILE-UPS ON THE PSYCHIC FREEWAY

The question of how gendered states of consciousness are possible has usually been countered with one of two assertions. Neither of them is very useful.

The first is the existence of a gendered identity. In my situation, this would mean that I felt like a man but sought to experience myself as a woman: my gender identity was female but my physical sex was male. Furnishing me with a gender identity does not, however, provide an explanation for internal subjective states. It simply presumes precisely what I'm trying to illuminate, namely, how it's possible for subjective bodily experiences to happen at all. How can my experience become stabilized and gendered in the first place?

This argument encounters further difficulties. For instance, since I also felt tall, young, athletic, Caucasian, and slender, I would also need a length identity, a durational identity, an athletic identity, and so on, with all of them dashing about inside me, and piling up on the Psychic Freeway during emotional rush hours.

The second assertion advanced is that my body objectively has certain features, i.e., I actually *am* slender or young or male, and so I *feel* slender or young or male. This kind of straightforward, unexamined essentialism assumes that my subjective experience flows directly from my physical features. It fails to answer the same kind of questions. For instance, I might *be* tall, but how is it possible for me to *feel* tall?

In addition, it implies that all slender or female or young people share a distinct subjective experience, one which transcends their individual lives, their cultural, historical, and ethnic identities. Isn't this unrealistic? The essentialist position also fails to address the inevitability of error: suppose I feel young and good-looking but I'm not?

The success of any of these objections means one must argue that essentialism is true, yet somehow fails to work. Even worse, an essentialist position completely fails to explain my lesbian friend and her high heels. Since she is a woman, then feeling like a woman should not only be unproblematic and independent of her attire, it should be unavoidable.

So we return to the same questions. How is it possible for physical features and social identities to be transformed into subjective internal experiences? How is it possible to *feel* ourselves to *be* anything at all?

IMAGINED BODIES: THE IMPOSSIBILITY OF THE REAL

How can we find my *real* body? Does it exist? And what if there are differing accounts of it? Perhaps, just perhaps, I have no real body, because any understanding of my body comes via the construction of an imaginary body, one that is created from the reservoir of cultural signs. In this way Foucault called the body a "volume in perpetual disintegration."[2] It is a totality that every culture or epoch dismembers into various parts, giving each a meaning and a name, then stitching them back together into a pseudo and supposedly natural "whole." The debate over the literal construction of transbodies has effectively hidden and therefore legitimized this constructed nature of *all* bodies.

Since we've introduced the word *signs* here, a brief review of semiotics is in order. "A sign," said Charles Pierce, "is something which stands to somebody for something in some respect."[3] Thus, words are signs, but so are paintings, and even gestures, like saluting the flag.

Every sign can be thought of as composed of two parts: the symbol or picture, and its meaning. More formally, these parts are called the *signifier* and *signified.* But that kind of terminology gets real confusing, real quick. The picture of a horse, or the word *horse,* is the symbol, and that molasses-slow, four-legged equine that cost me fifteen bucks in the fifth at Aqueduct is the meaning. My pointing gesture is the symbol, and "you are about to get stung by this humongous and really pissed-off-looking insect" is the meaning. This all sounds perfectly charming as long as it's kept simple. But what if there are greater complexities? If, for example, *cunt* is the sign, what can we fix as its symbol? What as its meaning?

We'd all like to believe that there is a primary experience of our bodies which precedes language and our body's subsequent break-up into signs. But it's a difficult argument to make. By the time we grasp the body *as* a body, it's already been draped in an entire blanket of cultural meanings. The same goes for sensation. Even in that most primal sensation, pain, cultural meanings play a critical role. The pain experienced in S/M play shows this, as does the pain of running a marathon or giving birth.

When we think, when we perceive, we use and manipulate signs. Each era and each culture creates its own signs and meanings, thus effectively shaping its own version of reality. To think of our bodies at all requires we use such signs. Once we do, we're no longer dealing with any direct experience of our bodies, but with experience as mediated, as understood through cultural signs.

You'd assume from this discussion that there are lots of meanings for our bodies to have, a wide marketplace of meanings from which to choose. You'd also expect that we'd be able to shift meanings at any time. In fact, it should practically be impossible not to change meanings much of the time, for if bodies have no fixed and predetermined meaning, stabilizing one should be pretty difficult.

TURN LEFT AT THE NEXT SIGN

In reality, this isn't the way things work. We've discussed the gender system using the body as "a site of constraint and authorization." This means it uses the constructed "natural" body to constrain certain feelings ("big boys don't cry"), while authorizing others ("don't you look sweet in your new dress?"). Thus, the gender system marks out what bodies can mean, regulates those meanings, and punishes transgression. This starts to address my first question about how it is possible to "feel like" anything at all, why our subjective experiences of our bodies don't just rush off in all directions at once, refusing to center or congeal into any particular experience.

One insight we can gain from semiotics is that the gender system doesn't have to punish to enforce its will. Recall Foucault's observation that power not only restrains, it creates. We live and think in a system of signs which by itself significantly shapes the meanings we can give our bodies. For instance, when a friend said to me, "I'd like to get surgery to eliminate this manly bulge that shows in a tight dress," my response was to ask how she knew the bulge was "manly." But the meaning that goes with the symbol of that bulge and makes the sign *penis* includes "manly, potent, and virile." It's hard to think of a *penis* as *penis* without connecting in some fundamental way with the concept of "masculinity."

The sign itself acts as a significant constraint on the ways in which we can conceive of that particular portion of flesh. It is this forcible shaping of our perception of our bodies within an inevitably heterosexist and binarist sign system that de Beauvoir calls "a criminal act, perpetrated by one class against another. It is an act carried out at the level of concepts, philosophy, politics."[4] It requires, as Judith Butler notes, "that the speaking subject, in order to speak, participate in the very terms of that oppression."[5]

For me, this means that "thinking" my body at all implicates me in my own self-oppression. The very signs I use to think about my body—my penis, breasts, semen—also render them completely unintelligible and strange. What should be a source of constant exploration of my innermost feelings is, instead, placed beyond my grasp. My body should be the one safe place to which I can turn in answering the questions life poses for us all: What is it I bring here? What will I leave behind? Answering these questions becomes for me a kind of physical as well as logical impossibility.

You can watch this participation in self-oppression at work within the transcommunity itself. Language has given us a kind of original, structural difference between nontransexuals and transexuals. Now transpeople themselves, while seeking furiously to narrow the social gap between themselves and nontransexuals, continually re-architect the original difference. This is done through the use of a series of terms, both invented and imported for the occasion, including *genetic girl, real woman, biological woman,* and *born woman.*

Yet the problem I have is not so much that the meanings are anathema to me. I recognize that the basic vocabulary of binarist meanings, of masculine and feminine, is reductionist, and enforced in an oppressive manner. But I personally don't seek meanings outside of that binarist system; I only seek to blend and merge its parts. What causes me pain is having my body read against me. The way I am asked to feel, think, and interact places precisely those meanings I want to bring into the world, and leave behind, out of my reach.

To go into this in any depth, we need to first grasp how I could understand what feeling "masculine" meant. Let's step back a moment to the time when—without knowing the word—I learned about "feminine." Let's start, where all good philosophy does, with my mother's bra.

ABREAST OF THE TIMES

I was about six when I discovered breasts. I had seen chests before but I did not yet recognize bosoms. My mother and my Aunt Peg were in the bedroom getting ready for a big family dinner. Not thinking to send me out, they began changing clothes. I'd seen chests before, though never a bra. The bra enabled me to recognize "breasts."

I watched them in the mirror, excited and struggling to understand as subtly as a six-year-old can stare without appearing to stare. In other words, I probably appeared transfixed, but they were kind enough to pretend not to notice. Mom and Peg were wearing these strange, lacy white harnesses. While they clearly functioned to hold their chests stationary, to me it seemed they were intended to do much more.

These were not what you would call practical or casual garments. This told me that what they contained must have very special social significance. These harnesses were intricately worked, with lace and little flowers in the design and many tiny curlicues. They were clearly meant to be looked at, to attract attention to these body parts. The effect was of something intended to be found enticing and alluring. In addition, the bright white cotton suggested innocence and purity to me, while the lace suggested softness or vulnerability.

This information was confusing to me. It didn't square with what

I knew about either my mother or my aunt. Both were strong-willed, mature, and substantial women. I didn't conceive of them, nor any portion of them, as soft, vulnerable, or enticing, yet the lacy, detailed construction of these garments made clear that they thought of their chests in this way. And anyone looking, as I was now, was meant to think of them that way as well.

These weren't particularly clandestine garments; after all, they were showing them to me, and to each other. On the other hand, since they wore them under their street clothes, being allowed to view them was apparently an act of some intimacy. The fact that they both wore them made me suspect that other women did so as well. So seeing women's chests as soft and vulnerable, enticing and alluring, was, therefore, probably a matter of general social agreement.

All of this constituted a kind of nonverbal dialogue between the three of us about their bodies. The fact that the door was closed, that they wore these things regularly under their clothes but seldom showed them, told me that this was a very intimate dialogue. This was my first conscious experience with the hiding and displaying of bodies and their various parts as a means of creating intimacy, and I found it exciting. Without ever having experienced desire, I was beginning to comprehend it: in discovering breasts, I had also begun to discover femininity and, with it, the concept of eroticism.

My second lesson, occurring at about the same time, came from my father, who taught me to look up girls' skirts. He had been complaining about short skirts over dinner, and I asked why he cared. He stared incredulously at me, suspicious that he was being put on. Reassured from my expression that I was perfectly serious, he snorted that, of course, everyone likes to look up women's skirts, because of what you could "see up there."

Now it was my turn to be incredulous. "Why in the world," I asked, "would anyone want to look at cotton panties? What is so exciting about them?" If I was so interested, I could see my fill in my sister's dresser drawer or in the women's section of any department store.

"It's what's behind them that makes it exciting," he said, explaining what he believed to be self-evident.

"But," I responded, "you're not looking at what's behind it." In truth, I hadn't a clue what was behind it, except that it was something I wasn't supposed to see. "In any case, you can see more with the girls on the beach in those bikinis. What's the big deal?"

The conversation broke down with him thinking I was either stupid or deliberately obtuse, probably both. The upshot was that I learned to look up women's skirts. After all, something very important was up there. If you were supposed to look at the white cotton over it, well, that must be some kind of intimate, exciting thing to do.

I spent the better part of second grade sitting directly across from Karen Masur, who was careful to stretch her skirt so tautly and primly across her legs that I could see right up it. To this day, if someone's skirt blows up like Marilyn's in *The Seven-Year Itch*, I know I'm going to look. I still don't know exactly why, but I know I will.

Now that we've made some progress in explaining how I learned what femininity was, we can move on to my education about what my body meant.

BUT EARLIER THAT SAME DAY, OVER ON THE SWINGSET...

I'd been playing in the sandbox during recess and looked up to see "Sweeta" Silverman on the swingset. Her real name was Cecile, but everyone called her Sweeta. I do not make this up. In fact, I finally ran into Sweeta again at our twentieth high school reunion and recounted this whole story.

Anyway, Sweeta was dressed in a nice white jumper, lace leggings, and little patent leather shoes. She wouldn't have lasted a minute in that sandbox. All us guys were dressed in heavy dungarees, sneakers, and other guy-type wear. We weren't color coordinated, we weren't clean, and we weren't supposed to be. The teacher certainly didn't lift us out of the sandbox like we were fragile pieces of china the way she carried Sweeta off that swingset when the bell rang. I envied her immediately.

I read the signs as clearly as if they'd been written on paper: the auguries were not good. I understood what her body meant and, in the same instant, I knew my father would make mincemeat of me if I wanted to dress like Sweeta, act like Sweeta, or be treated like Sweeta. He was certainly not going to treat me like valuable china—more like disposable plastic—and he'd have to stand in line behind all the boys in my class to do it. The bottom line was that my body was not going to have those meanings I associated with Sweeta, and I was going to have no say in the matter whatsoever.

What is interesting and sad is that even though no one actually told me what my body meant, it didn't make much difference. Signs don't mean anything in isolation. They only take on a meaning in relation to one another. In a gender system, the relations are always binary. By learning that my body could not mean what Sweeta's did was more than sufficient to tell me a great deal about what my body *must* mean.

In case you're wondering, yes, they treated me well at the reunion, and Sweeta was marvelous about the whole thing. Then again, she hasn't seen this book.

THROW DOWN YOUR MEANINGS AND GIVE YOURSELF UP

As I've grown older, I've spent many an evening trying to figure out why I couldn't just fight the language, no matter what my body meant. Why I couldn't create my own understanding of it, like a private language, the kind schizophrenics sometimes create. I've slowly realized there are several reasons why this was not possible.

The first is that I am not unhappy with the gendered alternatives, only with the way they are administered. Culture determines what my body means, and the meaning has to be completely one thing or another. Movement, mix and match, are strictly prohibited. This is like living in a straightjacket. So when people ask me if transexuality is learned or genetic, I conjure up the strangest image. I see them moving around in their straightjackets, hopping about with great concern. Then, noticing me with my arms free, they ask, "Are loose arms learned or genetic? Wouldn't you rather be normal?" Thank you, no.

The second reason why fighting the language is not the solution is that Foucault was right: the body may not be a stable basis for recognition. The meanings must be created and reinforced over and over, throughout one's life. Although recognizing one's body is impossible, it is, nonetheless, imperative. For me to navigate culture, for me to survive within it, I am compelled to recognize what others see in my body. I must acknowledge the hand of society pressed heavily upon my shoulder.

Most people master this recognition in childhood. They know what their bodies look like and accept the signs they learn to represent it without question. For transpeople, who completely shift registers of social recognition, the process has to be relearned, rehearsed, and recast.

When people started reading me as a woman, I had to very consciously learn how they saw me in order to use the restroom. I had to learn to recognize my voice, my posture, the way I appeared in clothing. I had to master an entire set of bathroom-specific communicative behaviors just to avoid having the cops called. In essence, I had to build an elaborate mental representation of how I looked and was read. And in spite of all this effort, sometimes it didn't work. The cops would humiliate me, checking my ID as publicly as possible, making sure everyone got a good, long look at the gendertrash being put back in its place—which was out of sight.

But my problem is not only avoiding social punishment, although failure to do so can result in humiliation, physical assault, even death. Building an "accurate" imaginary body, which maps closely to the social reading of my body, is critical to navigating social space. It's integral to knowing which clothes to wear, who I can ask for a date, how to get my hair cut, when to go on a diet, whether the ballet turn I just executed was sloppy or graceful, if I'm displaying a pleasant smile when you're talking to me, how to show the stranger on the street I don't want to be panhandled or the stranger at the bar I'm not interested in his buying me a drink.

With all this said, I'd like to think it's possible to negotiate the cultural labyrinth while still maintaining a private understanding. I used to wonder why I didn't just give the devil his due, form my own comprehension of myself, and go my own way—all the while learning to act appropriately in public. I have known a few exceptional souls who've been able to do this. They are very brave, very resourceful. For me, it was impossible.

One additional factor I have had to take into account is that I have always borne the curse of so many abuse survivors—a terrible emotional transparency. The language of signs which enfolds each of our bodies communicates what's inside us too clearly for our own good.

JUST KEEP IT TO YOURSELF

If the body is always a sign being read, then not communicating is impossible. One's body continues to display a multitude of information through nonlinguistic signs, the languages of gesture, posture, stance, and clothing. How could it be possible to feel feminine or masculine and not communicate it in every moment for the world to read? Whenever I felt the things I saw on Sweeta, the visible language of my posture, gesture, and vocal inflection said it as clearly as if I wore it in big letters across my chest.

While it certainly is possible for some people to hide their feelings, not many of us can do it for very long, certainly not for a lifetime. And in childhood, every day is an entire lifetime, a month an eternity. The ability to hide feelings, using bodily clues to misdirect or obscure, is usually something learned in adulthood.

Since hiding my feelings wasn't possible, I did the next best thing: I learned not to feel at all. I displayed either active disinterest, aggression, or anger. All displays were meant to keep people at a distance, to protect me from discovery. They worked. They formed the basis of my emotional vocabulary and sustained me until I was nineteen. By then I had left home, hearth, and friends for a succession of far-off places where complete anonymity assured me that my body would be of little interest to anyone.

My first and best lesson in emotional camouflage came in the boys' locker-rooms. It was normal to engage in pecking-order displays, like the put-down fights in which we insulted each other's mothers and sisters with the lewdest possible lines. Cries of, "Hey, Johnson, I butt-fucked your sister!" had to be rejoined with, "Yeah, and after your mom got done sucking my dick I let her off her knees and handed back her quarter."

Failing to participate in these verbal assaults meant risking being branded a queer. It meant winding up a sexual suspect. I had to be on my guard every day, all day, for as long as I was at that school. And no parent, no teacher, no friend was going to protect me from it. I was in danger and I knew it. Seeya would have to wait.

Within the closed world of those locker-rooms, three times a week, every week of the school year, year in and year out, I practiced being male and masculine. It was a matter of building a mental representation of myself that expressed itself in my posture, voice, and stance. In other words, by putting the right signs in my head.

If I went numb and cold, if I concentrated on envisioning myself as muscular, angry, and aggressive, I could get by. Guys would leave me alone. The harassment stopped. It was replaced by respect, or at least distance, which was all I wanted from them. Actually, it was what I preferred. I had learned to be a "boy."

With hindsight, the funny thing is that I thought I could be such a tough character. The honest truth was, I didn't have a violent bone in my body. What aggression I had came out of my mouth. I became a complete smart-ass. That got me beat up a couple times, too. I found out many of the guys avoided me simply because they considered me a jerk. But it worked.

I kept those images in my head for years, that particular sense of myself. I still use it today when I'm out alone late at night and have to walk in a dangerous neighborhood, or I see someone sizing me up from across a darkened street. That self-image reemerges forcefully in my stride, in the way I hold myself, clench my fists, and scowl.

Survival came at a cost, however. It would take me eight years to begin recovering some of those feelings I had lost in that sandbox. I would spend entire evenings on my knees, crying and "chewing the carpet" as my childhood and adolescence came rushing back to me. Underneath what was numb there was pain. Sometimes I needed the numbness back, just to be able to pull on my clothes and get to work.

YOU CAN ALWAYS FALL OFF A HORSE, BUT IT MAY NOT BE A HORSE WHEN YOU GET BACK ON

My original question about how it's possible to feel oneself as *anything* arrives here. The subjective experience of gender, as well as being read or experienced by another as gendered, is not a *being*, but a *doing*. It is performed anew each time. It is the thrill of friction, of the possibility of the performance going awry, being destabilized, misappropriated, that accounts for the fascination with— and fear of—transpeople.

Culture's greatest magic trick is convincing us that reading a body as gendered requires something inside which that body is or has, and which expresses itself through gendered acts. The reading of gender onto bodies is, in itself, a gendered act. One might say it is the gendering act. The imaginary bodies created by such readings are not the origins of gender but their result.

This process accounts for our confusion when discussing gendered bodies in general and transbodies in particular. We mistake what we read on such bodies for a reality *in* these bodies—one which precedes, and is therefore independent of, our reading. Thus, transbodies serve as an extended Rorschach test. The way people read our bodies is eerily reminiscent of the joke where the subject who sees sex in every single inkblot is finally confronted by the shrink and then protests, "But *you're* the one with all the dirty pictures."

If gender is something composed of acts, both the act of performing gender and the action of reading that performance, then in each moment there is also the small possibility of change, of movement, of reading the map "incorrectly." There is the possibility of transgression and difference. For although gender is an effective system, it's not perfect; otherwise, I wouldn't be here.

READING IN THE DARK

Changing what I "meant" required my learning to use a particular set of internal signs to create myself, to re-read my own body. I believe this performance of internal visualization, of manipulating signs, is what makes it possible for me to be anything. It is what makes it possible for me to feel "like a woman," or sometimes "like a man," sometimes like in-between, and sometimes like nothing at all. It is what makes it possible for my lesbian-feminist friend to feel "like a natural woman," and for Aretha to sing about it.

The images we form of ourselves and see in our heads constitute a kind of internal dialogue. They are conversations we hold with ourselves about what our bodies mean, an imaginary construction we undertake over and over again. In time, these images stabilize and become what we identify as "our selves."

These signs usually do not have clear pictures, but the meaning is always clear. For instance, imagine a body/sign you know well, perhaps Marilyn Monroe. Although you may have seen her image scores of times, chances are, the symbol or picture is pretty fuzzy. What it means, however, remains vivid. The sign "works" as a whole. It is not that her body necessarily means anything at all, but each time you perform that meaning, you re-create her as well. It is the stability of this performance that creates an identifiable "Marilyn" for you. Many people, myself among them, do that with our selves.

In the locker-room, I learned to keep a sign in my head for my body. Its meaning was hard, masculine, and angry. It was not easy for a good Jewish boy to do, but it was sufficient for me to survive and pass as male.

But feelings do not go away; they just go underground. Those feelings that were native to me didn't disappear. They reappeared— on other bodies. To experience "feminine" I went in search of bodies where I could safely have feminine feelings. I spent years sleeping with as many women as possible when I reached adulthood. I did this not because I was turned on or wanted sex, but because, within that environment, it was safe for me to have that particular subjective experience, even if I had to locate it as happening on someone else's body.

It seems that while we are capable of experiencing different gendered states, most of us identify with only one of those as "us." This means that only certain identifications harmonize with how we want to be in the world—what we want to bring, what we want to leave behind.

This process of identification was disastrous for me. The meanings with which I was allowed to identify, as well as the way my body was read by others, was inverted and painful. So I acted out sexually, trying to both escape that pain and re-own something lost inside me long, long ago. The process of unlocking my misery, of getting my body "back," has been neither brief nor easy. What I see in the mirror still occasionally distresses me: at times I see the "me" in the locker-room, and it hurts.

Ultimately, it is to that person in the mirror that we must take the fight against a gender regime. Of course we need to struggle in the streets, in homes and churches, schools and jobs, state and federal capitols. Finally, though, we must struggle in our own hearts, for it is here that a gender system first regulates who and what we can "be." To reinvent and re-gender yourself is a tall order. In the words of Fritz Perls, "To die and be reborn is not an easy thing."[6]

DE-GENDERING SOCIETY

A friend once said to me that all this was about Buddhism, about transcending the self. The problem of my male self would be resolved when I transcended the very ideas of "self" and "gender" and merged with the greater Oneness. This echoes the notion that transpeople should somehow aim to be "genderfree," as if that were a possible, or desirable, goal.

No doubt for some it is. For me, it is not. Eroticizing bodies almost inevitably leads to gendering them in some fashion, and then to a system that regulates them. A gender regime enforces five basic laws: (1) there are only two cages; (2) everyone must be in a cage; (3) there is no mid-ground; (4) no one can change; and (5) no one chooses their cage.

I want just three things: (1) the right to choose my own meanings—including none at all; (2) a freer marketplace from which to choose; and (3) freedom from the constant threat of punishment for my choices. That's all.

Many of us, both trans and nontrans, are not interested in transcending or relinquishing our selves, but in being very particular and specific selves, ones which give meaning and resonance to our lives. It is this search that leads each of us down the varied spiritual paths we travel, hoping to find ourselves at the end, sitting quietly in that primeval playground—happy and alive and waiting.

1. Michel Foucault, *Language, Counter-Memory, Practice: Selected Essays and Interviews* (Ithaca, NY: Cornell University Press, 1977), p. 153.

2. Ibid., p. 148.

3. Charles Pierce in *Semiotics: An Introductory Anthology,* edited by Robert Innes (Bloomington, IN: Indiana University Press, 1985), p. 1.

4. Simone de Beauvoir in Monique Wittig, "The Mark of Gender," *Feminist Issues 5,* no. 2 (Fall 1985): 5.

5. Judith Butler, *Gender Trouble* (New York: Routledge, 1990), p. 116.

6. Fritz Perls, *Gestalt Therapy Verbatim* (Lafayette, CA: Real People Press, 1969), author's epigraph.

EROTICISM: ON THE USES OF DIFFERENCE

THERE IS A COUPLE I PLAY WITH from time to time. The woman seems to adore my body, yet she almost invariably refers to me as *he* and *him*. We've discussed how she eroticizes my body, although the language for such discussions is sparse at best. I have gleaned that, while she nominally considers me a woman, in bed she nonetheless perceives me as a special kind of man.

Her husband, on the other hand, is a devastatingly sweet and gentle Latino who has never had a sexual experience with another man. He vows that he never will. The idea that I am anything but a woman is completely foreign to him, even confusing. He invariably refers to me as *she* and *her*.

Neither of them finds his and her differing views of my body dissonant. But what do they see there, and how is it possible for both of them to have such "conflicting" eroticizing experiences simultaneously? Surely my body doesn't feel different to one than to the other, and isn't eroticism about the physical sensations of sex? Or is something else at work here?

WHAT DO YOU SAY TO A NAKED HERM?

Michel Foucault once pointed out that our culture has made of sexual pleasure a pseudoscience, surrounding it with a legion of courts, doctors, sociologists, churches, and shrinks. All of them undertake to manage our sexuality, in large part by obligating members of society to search out and pronounce some kind of inner truth from their erotic pleasures.

This is by way of contrast with other cultures' more sensible approach, in which sexual knowledge is founded on an erotics arts, on pleasure itself—how to produce, maximize, and prolong it.[1] For an erotic arts there are no hidden secrets, trapdoors, or rabbits concealed in the carnal hat. Sex is not about truth but enjoyment, and there is no knowledge to be mined from pleasure but its magnification.

As compelling as this approach seems, it doesn't quite work. An erotic arts seems straightforward at first glance. After all, what could be simpler than sexual pleasure, especially when set against the elaborate structure with which we've surrounded it?

On closer inspection, however, discontinuities appear. For instance, there are many lesbians who have stared at me in a kind of mute admiration (there is no accounting for taste), rooted to the spot as I watch them strip their mental gears, wondering what my body means and what they will find in my pants. They are not, I trust, worried about sensation itself. Rather, they are concerned with meaning: how they would eroticize me or whatever we might do together, if, indeed, they could eroticize me at all.

They need not have felt so conflicted about it; after all, I've experienced some of the same problems myself. For it is precisely when the rules "fail" on erotically queered bodies—men with one-inch penises, hermaphrodite bodies with different (and possibly better) genital formations, women with penises or constructed vaginas, men in dresses—that we become aware of rules to begin with. Without eroticism, our discussion of gender so far would be mostly relegated to aesthetics, i.e., what the best ways are to understand bodies—as if we were discussing painting or sculpture.

Discussions about queer bodies don't feel that way though.

For no matter what sophisticated arguments are advanced about essentializing biological sex or gender, it all comes back to desire. The very idea of degendering bodies (were that possible *or* desirable), or of proliferating genders ad infinitum, produces in many of us a sense of vertigo, even nausea. Participating in the erotic economy seems to require gender. Kate Bornstein may be right that it's not sane to call a rainbow black or white,[2] but when it comes to arousal, most of us do not yet own color sets. Unlike other animals, we lack the capacity to go into heat or to enjoy specific cycles of rutting, so that the attachment of arousal to specific bodies, organs, and meanings seems less like some deep, inner drive and more like something in the nature of a cultural achievement.

This becomes more apparent with bodies that refuse to play by the rules. Erotically queered bodies open uncomfortable questions: What turns us on? How would we negotiate the construction of intimacy and arousal with a fully different Other? It seems most people find gender-unintelligible bodies to be erotically unintelligible as well. Thus it may be that a prime reason for the extraordinary, almost deranged level of violence visited on transpeople, especially in intimate situations, is not that we transgress gender, but rather that we transgress eroticism, a far more visceral and incendiary thing. This makes many of us feel like our moorings for sexual arousal are being stripped away.

As indeed they are. For when all the intellectual parlor games are over, when we still go home and jerk off to *Playboy, Playgirl, BlueBoy, Tran-Fan, On Our Backs* ("Entertainment for the Adventurous Lesbian"), *On Your Knees!* (Entertainment for the Submissive Lesbian), and *Kennels & Runs* (Entertainment for the Depraved Lesbian), eroticism begins to look like the anchor stabilizing the whole project of gender. Eroticism is not the fixative of sexual intimacy between two gendered subjects, nor the pleasure they produce, but what grounds the very idea of two gendered subjects in the first place. It is an erotic economy based on difference that actually requires a gender regime in the first place, i.e., the creation and regulation of difference, and an erotics of difference is the basic means by which desire is made to happen on other people's bodies—the first requirement for procreation.

So, bearing in mind that there is a special place in Hell reserved for first approximations, I will argue that it is not that our culture lacks an erotic arts of its own. Far from it. Rather it is that, although we believe in a "natural" erotics of sensation and sex, in fact we have constructed an elaborate and extensive cultural erotics based almost entirely upon the meaning and difference of bodies.

RIKSTER IN HEAT

I'm standing outside looking around and I spot someone walking down the street with tight blue jeans, a cute butt, and long swaying blond hair. Nice set of signs there: visions of soft, young genderbunnies dance in my head. Suddenly, the person turns the corner and I see the full beard and lean chest. The genderbunny vanishes, only to be replaced by the thought of a neo-hippie guy, probably into heavy metal, dope, and dormitories filled with nubile female bodies. What happened?

The symbols stayed the same. The tight jeans, butt, and hair remain unchanged, but the meaning of these symbols has shifted for me. Put another way, I'm performing a different set of meanings on that body. And if I'm later introduced to that person as a female-to-male transexual, chances are I'll reorganize the meanings yet again. For that matter, if he/she turns out to be Jennifer Miller, who performs as "The Bearded Lady," doubtless I'll go through yet another reorganization.

BELIEVING IS SEEING

It was in one of our local trans-support groups that I noticed a mustachioed, quite heavyset young man, sitting quietly to one side. I clocked the broad manner, heavyweight wristwatch, masculine postures, and, although you never want to prejudge anyone, I couldn't help thinking that he was likely to have a rather rough and trying time living as a woman. I thought we would probably see quite a lot of him in the future as he'd need lots of support: no one was going to easily identify this person as a woman. All of which was neither intended to be pro or con—just an observation.

Of course, before the evening was over he shared with us that he was a male transexual, was currently contemplating phalloplasti (penis-construction surgery), and had been living as a man for years. He talked briefly about some personal issues and left, never to return. As he spoke, I, cosmopolitan that I am, watched in amazement as my eyes raced back over his body and re-encoded everything I saw there to support what I now knew. Doubtless had he told me afterward that it was all a joke, I would have re-encoded everything once again, then fallen to the floor in a postmodern frenzy.

A DIFFERENCE ENGINE

Every direction this book has turned is to have been confronted with difference. It is as if every body, physical act, gesture, and article of clothing is read through a dumb Rosetta stone that translates each symbol into one of two meanings, or a flawed prism through which we all look that defracts all incoming images into one of only two colors.

What I would like to argue here is that gender, loosely defined, is this difference engine we keep coming at from a variety of angles: a set of cultural technologies for producing stabilizing differences between bodies. Its binding principle is not just the formal systems (laws, courts, medicine, etc.), nor the techniques of discipline and self that produce and uphold our belief in it, but its peculiar and peculiarly powerful ability to secure itself, to stabilize and even create eroticism.

Our erotics is about a specific sort of pleasure, a gendered pleasure. It is not the pleasure of bodies, but pleasure in the meaning of bodies, and not just pleasure in the meaning of bodies, but pleasure in the difference of bodies. Most specifically, it is in the difference of power between bodies as read through binaries like hard/ soft, active/passive, strong/weak, dominating/submitting, virile/fertile, thrusting/accepting, penetrating/penetrated, and unyielding/ vulnerable.

Many readers will assume that I am talking about butch-femme or heterosexual couples. But eroticism is not what *attracts* us to desirable bodies—it is what *constitutes* them. As transbodies illustrate, this construction is both coercive and unstable, so that with genderqueer bodies, erotic meanings are not just *there,* but must be negotiated. Thus an "obviously" butch-femme couple may read themselves as butch-butch, femme-femme, femme-butch, or something else entirely. And even the garden-variety heterosexual couple may not be reading themselves as male-female, let alone as heterosexual.

THE TRAFFIC IN MEANING

Here I'd like to appropriate shamelessly from Gayle Rubin's landmark "The Traffic in Women,"[3] which explains culture's sexual division of labor as existing "to ensure the union of men and women by making the smallest viable economic unit contain at least one man and one woman." Or, as Lévi-Strauss put it, "the sexual division of labor is nothing else than a device to institute a reciprocal state of dependency between the sexes."[4]

Assuming we all start life with a full semiotic deck of meanings, in order to be created or to create ourselves as one set of meanings, we must lose access to some others. If you want to play with or experience the masculinity of bodies, you need a boy-type unit, and if you want to play with or experience the femininity of bodies, you need a girl-type unit. The effect of this is that the smallest complete set of gendered meanings is always one man and one woman. The binary division of the sexes turns out to be nothing more or less that a device to ensure a reciprocal state of dependency between what are now two types of bodies.

The primary way to recover the "lost" parts is through the intensive intimacy of erotic desire. In fact, if you spend any time watching people having sex (and I confess to having passed scores of hours this pleasant way), you soon come to the conclusion that people are eroticizing a vicarious enjoyment of that lost part. Men are not just eroticizing their own masculinity, but also vicariously enjoying the vulnerability of women, and vice versa.

A moment's reflection reveals that, for a man, even to enjoy one's own masculinity requires one to first experience a prior femininity, against which it can be perceived. Paradoxically, then, men who are busy ogling large breasts are not enjoying women's "femininity" (they have no idea what she might be experiencing, if anything), but rather, they are producing the aesthetic experience of femininity in themselves, something which they then must disown as "not me," as coming from outside themselves.

WAS IT MEANINGFUL FOR YOU, HONEY?

If any of this is true, we might be moved to ask why meaning has assumed such a central position in our culture's erotics. What is the social utility of promoting a traffic in meaning rather than sensation? To begin with, sensation is an inherently unstable foundation for such an enterprise: it's private, difficult to code into words and images, and it doesn't travel very well. It requires direct physical contact for its effect, rather like trying to describe to someone what bacon cooking smells like, or how it feels to get stoned.

In short, sensation requires a lot of bandwidth and is difficult to direct. Meaning, on the other hand, has every advantage: it is part and parcel of words and images, and can be completely public, mass-produced, and mass-distributed. And unlike sensation, which requires all the enormous bandwidth of human contact, you can get an entire meaning into a word, a sentence, a single picture. Meaning is particularly well-suited for our electronic world.

Just check any cybersex chat room where entirely immaterial but inevitably gendered bodies exchange an endless pleasure in the meanings of their virtual bodies. Try imagining an Internet, a Times Square billboard, or some other mass medium of communication which could carry direct physical sensation back and forth, and you begin to appreciate the scale of the difficulties in organizing the field of desire around an erotics based on sensation.

Looking at the congestion of sexualized images we now inhabit, it may be that as a culture we have reached some kind of developmental apex in detaching pleasure from sensation, while simultaneously saturating our semantic environment with the pleasures of meaning. One wonders if we have not begun to take pleasure simply in desire itself, rather than its satisfaction, a desire which, since it lacks any attachment to satiation, is infinitely manipulated, massaged, and magnified.

IT WAS GOOD, BUT NOT SENSATIONAL

If we really eroticized sensation, there'd be an entire art devoted solely to self-recreation, since most of us are going to experience more pleasure from ourselves during our lifetimes than from any other source—probably by an order of magnitude. But then every February 14th we'd all be writing Valentine's Day cards to our right hand saying, "Miss you. Wish you were here. Ooops. You are here. Have to run; something's just come up." Of course, some people would insist on addressing such cards to their left hands, and we would rightfully denounce them as perverts.

Unlike an erotics of sensation, which might wander about with no purpose but to amplify itself, an order of erotics based on meaning has a domesticating effect: it points desire and arousal outward, toward other people's bodies, in particular toward those organs, acts, and bodies that are procreatively useful. A specifically gendered pleasure is generally thought of as a useful thing; it is pleasure made productive. This happens while erasing or ignoring those bodies, acts, and physical sites that contradict it.

If you're a Wall Street broker and you put on a three-thousand-dollar Armani hand-stitched silk suit in the morning and it makes you feel so virile that when you go into work you get an erection and want to fuck every secretary on the trading floor, you're a stud. But if you go home that night and put on a three-thousand-dollar Armani hand-stitched backless silk gown and it makes you feel so feminine when you look in the mirror that you get an erection and jerk off, you're a pervert. You'll have plenty of trouble finding partners, or even naming and explaining your pleasures. This is not because of the activity in which you engaged, but because only some acts and signs are allowed to qualify as erotic.

The primary technique of our erotics is not prohibition, as in forbidding specific acts, but the creation of specific sites, acts, and bodies as erotic currency in the first place, simultaneously making others unintelligible, even unthinkable.

Our erotics has created an entire Geography of the Absent—body parts that aren't named, acts one mustn't do, genders one can't perform—because they are outside the binary box. We live in an erotics peopled by ghosts we cannot see and are haunted, nonetheless, by the specter of their return: the naked genderqueer body which—fully clothed in our discomfort and confusion—reveals that it is our gender wearing no clothes. Erotically queer bodies don't "float free." It is, rather, the project of annexing erotic meanings to bodies that floats free, queering the entire enterprise.

Yet this profoundly political system successfully masquerades as some primordial force bubbling up from deep inside us, like Jed Clampett's oil well, a fiction well-secured by the discomfort many of us feel when contemplating other ways to organize arousal. Perhaps, as Foucault suggests, we ought to be less concerned with the familiar liberal project of freeing our erotic pleasures from cultural restraint, and begin inquiring how we have been taxed with a specific erotic system to begin with.

As Foucault exhorted his readers to conceive of "power without the throne," so we must begin to conceive of an erotics without sensation—an erotics that is not what we feel when someone rubs our pants, but the erotics flashed daily across our mental screens. What is eroticized increasingly bears only the most tangential and tenuous relationship to the actualities of copulation and its sensations. Our erotic arts have become more deeply embedded in the pleasures we take in what bodies mean rather than how they feel.

Yet even with our prevailing and apparently interminable fascination with how gender and so-called biological sex are constructed (to which this book contributes), the cultural construction of pleasure and eroticism has been largely bypassed by "serious" theorists as either so embarrassingly personal or intractably natural that it is better left to those feminists engaged in the ritual denunciations of porn, or those queer theorists practicing deep deconstruction on the last Tom of Finland catalog or the next issue of *Mandate*.

I May Not Know Deconstruction But I Know What Gives Me a Hard-on, Damnit!

Okay. Now I know someone out there is grumbling, "This dumb-ass sex-change is now going to tell me nothing is erotic." First of all, don't call me names. They hurt my dumb-ass sex-change feelings. The lament that arguments about desire ignore that we "really do" have pleasures, or bodies, misses the point. Of course we have pleasures and bodies. What I'm trying to pose is a somewhat different set of concerns, questions about which pleasures and what bodies are allowed to circulate as the basis of exchange for intimacy and arousal.

I am also not saying that we don't get aroused. I am asking instead how it is that we come to recognize some acts, bodies, and pleasures as erotic to begin with. What are the rules by which the entire project of eroticism can occur so that we can even discuss such a thing? How is it that I moved from the simple pleasure of playing with myself after school each day to the very different and culturally loaded act of "masturbating"? And when and how did this mutate into something associated less with feeling than with other bodies?

I am less interested (except in a prurient way) in what gets us off individually than in what is supposed to get us off. How do we come to understand "getting off" as a specific thing to begin with? What kinds of activities are legitimated for "getting off," and what are the effects on those activities that are left out or left unaddressed? It is not so much that if we eroticized sheep, people would beat off over lamb chops, but rather that eating lamb chops would be considered beating off.

Not All Produce Is Production

Looking into eroticism is a difficult enterprise on several counts. First, we are used to having our pleasures politicized and negated. Thus, the lesbian-feminist analysis of sex in the early 1980s results in that strangest of oxymorons—"politically correct sex," which can be shortened to the acronym BORING. This roughly translates to sex that takes place side by side (not into roles), at the same time (you are both equally important), with your lover (no tricking), while eschewing both penetration (male-identified) and fantasies (signs of oppression) and enjoying the strains of Holly Near singing about the evils of nuclear power.

Certainly no one who owns a vibrator and has a bowl of country-fresh vegetables, as I do, would want to deny us our own particular pleasures. Does this mean, however, that any inquiry into the general scheme of erotics that our culture has constructed must have as its goal issuing various proscriptions and prohibitions as to what "ought" to get us off?

The second difficulty, to paraphrase a recent article, is that writing about eroticism is a little like trying to describe a building while standing only a quarter of an inch away from it. You can see everything, and absolutely nothing, at the same time: it's all too close. Take nudity as an example.

The invention of nakedness (not not wearing clothes but rather the consciousness that one is "naked")—simply by hiding various body parts from view—creates the mere displaying and viewing of bodies as a medium of intimacy, a focus of desire, a point of arousal. We have developed a highly advanced methodology of concealing, exposing, teasing, and insinuation out of the basics of sight itself, and then deployed it relentlessly. Sight may be the easiest sense to organize in the service of procreative arousal. Yet we're so accustomed to such use, it often passes without notice.

YOUR ABSENCE IS SHOWING

Inquiring after eroticism entails seeing what is not there as well as seeing what is. As Foucault noted, there are many silences, not just one, each of them part of the entire discourse and each of them different. But in spite of the critical feminist injunction to the contrary, it is very hard to listen for silence or to see an absence.

This reminds me of the pictures on the wall in the gym where I work out. They are formal larger-than-life Greco-Roman drawings of male and female torsos. Both have nice, hard stomachs. Above the woman's, though, are jutting breasts with distinct, upturned—

if chaste—nipples. The man's chest has flat pecs (not breasts) with muscles, but with no nipples whatsoever.

I don't think these drawings are intended to be anatomically incorrect. I think they represent the way most of us see men's chests: they simply don't have nipples. Why? Because they aren't useful or necessary to what we want men's chests to mean. Nipples are sensitive and feminine, and thus an embarrassing contradiction to our concept of the masculinity of men's chests. We don't need to be restrained from seeing them; we simply choose not to.

It is kind of funny in this case, since this particular gym is located in Greenwich Village and is mostly populated by gay men who, even on a slow day, sometimes risk whiplash cruising the passing pecs and their little pink nipples.

Because our erotics is mainly based on shaping and molding desire by defining the terms under which it can proceed, rather than on a structure of repression and prohibition, it is often difficult to see what is missing. It is possible to disqualify the most elementary sexual practices from the erotic, not by being proscriptive but by erasing them, by directing attention elsewhere, and by employing a language that oppresses by obscuring rather than communicating.

I am not just trying to score esoteric Brownie points here at the Semiotic Bowl Games. It is impossible to walk into a women's bar, spot a hot number, and, sidling closer while smiling and blushing fetchingly (I've actually tried this part), say, "Hi, I'd like to go home with you and tribate."

We are in the throes of an explosion of queer sex books, but I've yet to find one that asks about the concepts it is forced to inhabit: What body parts are named, what acts, what kinds of penetration? What are the boundaries that define intercourse? How can we seriously engage a queer sexuality when to be sexual at all requires us to participate in a language of heterosexuality?

I JUST CAN'T RELATE TO THAT

And then, we are also used to thinking in terms of individual things, not relations. But our erotics is founded on power, difference, intimacy—all of which are relations. They happen between people and are not reducible to only one of them. This is part of what makes our erotics so socially useful: desire is attached to the requirement for another person.

Yet because the erotic, like gender, is not "in" either party alone but rather in the relationship between them, it runs counter to the way we generally analyze practices, which is by breaking them down. As the Germans were quick to tell us, you can't break down a gestalt; the whole is different from the sum of its parts. For instance, you can know a middle *C* and an *E* perfectly well, but that won't tell you anything about how the major-third *da-da-da-DUM* opening of Beethoven's *Fifth* sounds because "thirdness" is "neither in the *C* nor the *E*, nor does it depend on those particular notes." "No knowledge about the parts in isolation would ever give the remotest hint as to what ['thirdness'] is like."[5]

Which is to say, you can look at all the parts of an automobile spread across the garage floor, but that still won't tell you a single useful thing about a Ferrari rounding a turn at Le Mans at a hundred miles an hour. Need I add, I like to think that reducing my transgenitals to the details of their surgical alteration is about the same thing, although I don't corner quite as well at high speeds.

CLOSING THOUGHTS AND THIGHS

A transexual male friend gives a class discussion on his surgery. Afterward, a student inquires whether he can successfully have sex like a man, and he responds, "Yes, I can penetrate my lover and we can have simultaneous orgasm." Months later I read a sex piece by his lover in a national bisexual magazine. Unsure what to make of his one-inch penis, she devotes only a sentence or two to it, instead concentrating the bulk of the piece on his penetration of her with his fingers and how she can tell his absolute maleness from the deep, relentless way he fucks her for hours.

The erotic has acted as an injunction on what to hide and what to show, what to proffer freely and what to withhold, what can be exchanged for pleasure and what cannot. It even legitimizes what can count as pleasurable to begin with. It does this by attaching to bodies a pleasure in meaning, particularly a pleasure in difference and the gendered difference of power. Additionally, it excludes or erases those bodies, acts, and desires which do not meet its aims.

As long as we deal in an erotics whose source and origin is the different meanings between bodies as they relate to the binary of procreation, for just so long, genderqueer bodies like mine will remain erotically inaccessible and unintelligible, as well as socially at risk. We are trapped at the margins not of gender but of arousal, and for genderqueer bodies to be able to fully participate in the erotic economy, we must first be willing to examine the system which has successfully made such bodies preposterous, threatening, or even disgusting to so many.

1. Michel Foucault, *The History of Sexuality: An Introduction,* vol. 1 (New York: Vintage, 1990), p. 53.

2. Kate Bornstein, *Gender Outlaw* (New York: Routledge, 1994), p. 128.

3. Gayle Rubin, "Traffic in Women: Notes on the 'Political Economy' of Sex" in *Toward an Anthropology of Women,* edited by Rayna Reiter (New York: Monthly Review Press, 1975).

4. Claude Lévi-Strauss, *The Elementary Structures of Kinship* (Boston: Beacon Press, 1969), p. 480.

5. Carroll Pratt, Introduction to Wolfgang Kohler, *The Task of Gestalt Psychology* (Princeton, NJ: Princeton University Press, 1969), p. 10.

LINES IN THE SAND,
CRIES OF DESIRE

We are the women who like to come, and come hard.

Amber Hollibaugh

IN YOUR FACE, JOAN, IN YOUR FACE.

We spoke last week, just your average phone call. And then, as we're ringing off, you suggest I might want to write about the boundaries where my different selves meet: the complexity of this place, its borders and contours. Your suggestion leaves my face burning with shame and anger, as if I had been struck. Who has ever wanted to hear such things? Where on earth can a lesbian, a pre-operative transexual with a cock, a woman, a femme, an addict, an incest survivor, and a post-operative transexual with a cunt intersect? Upon what map is it drawn?

I have spent my life exploring the geography of this place, mastering unfamiliar terrain and alien customs, wandering regions as fresh, as uncharted, as inexplicable to me as private visions. I have surveyed its pathways, as ignorant and blind as any first-time explorer, and finally discovered myself at day's end—lost, alone, bewildered, and afraid. With time, my tracks have intersected and converged, crisscrossed again and again, until at last they have woven their own pattern: my life itself has become the place where these different selves meet, my skin the boundary that contains them, the women in my life the bordering states.

You say you want me to tell you about this place, its complexities and desires, its contours and terrain. It is 1:00 A.M. on Sunday morning, and at the moment I am more involved with the contours and terrain of the cock dangling about two inches in front of my face. I am forty-two, and I have been coming to this mostly straight, couples-only sex club in mid-Manhattan for almost a year now, working my way through acts successively more challenging and frightening for me, pushing back the boundaries of what I can do or imagine, practicing with newfound skill staying present and connected during sex, exorcising demons and ghosts by now so familiar I know their names and faces within an environment so anonymous I often don't know those of my partners. A place where straightforward sex is the commodity, physical beauty the currency, and lust the only coin. This is the ground I have chosen to confront my deep fear of butch or masculine sexuality, of possession and surrender, power and vulnerability, where I can finally recover the many, the myriad ways and fragments of my life lost to incest, transexuality, shame, and self-hate. I am trying to reclaim myself, and I want my body back.

I want my body back.

I want my clit, my scrotum, my vagina, my cock, my beard. My buttocks, my thighs, my bush, my asshole, my urethra, my semen. My lips, my tongue, my wetness, and my saliva. I want my breasts back, the ones I watched go through a second complete puberty at twenty-nine. I want my nipples back, with the scars just beneath my pink areolae where the implants went in, the left incision making the nipple over my heart mostly numb to touch or tongue. I want the scar on my throat, the one people notice and ask about my thyroid condition, the one opened to shave my Adam's apple down. And I want the scars you can't see, on the inside of my labia, the ones you get by doing the stitching from the inside so they don't show. The ones which ache when I'm getting ill and itch strangely when I'm getting exhausted.

I want my body back.

I want the clear ejaculate which still trickles from my urethra when I come hard and fast. I want my clit back, the one the supersurgeons, who can make almost anything into almost anything else, made by transplanting the very head, the glans, of my beautiful, long, ivory-pink-and-blue-veined penis right between my labia and then waiting three months for it to heal and the blood supply to stabilize, and then, in a second operation, carved down to the little clitlike apparatus I have now, which is somehow still so sensitive it makes me tense and shiver as the wife of the man with the cock dangling about two inches in front of my face uses her left hand to open my lips and her right to rub it inquiringly, watching my face closely for any reaction and then smiling in satisfaction when my eyes unfocus, my stomach muscles harden, and my thighs spread a little of their own accord.

In your face, Joan, in your face.

In my mouth goes his prick, tasting at first of latex and then nonoxynol-9, which makes my lips and tongue go bitter and numb. A little gag starting, and then he is in my mouth and firming up nicely, the glans beginning to extend itself along my tongue and pushing up against the roof of my palate. An exciting and strange experience this, but stranger still is that having had a cock, and having had women go down on it, I'm unwillingly, suddenly, almost shockingly aware of how each movement of my lips and tongue must feel to him. Strange, too, is that nerve endings which once made their home in my cock, and which now nestle in my cunt, are starting to remember too, and they're getting hot, turgid, and wet, and for several transcendent moments I cannot distinguish if I'm giving head to him, or to me.

He is fully erect now, much like my dildo, except the skin of his penis is very smooth, and gripping it with both hands, I feel an unexpected softness around a firm core. After a moment I begin turning on my hands and knees, moving around on the mattress to face his wife as we begin to kiss. Her black hair is loose and shoulder length, her mouth is soft and wet and opens to hard little biting edges which nip at my mouth, tongue, and neck. I notice the small, downy hairs on her forearm, damp, and glistening in the overhead light. Her muscles work as she reaches for my cunt again, the hairs turning blonde as they catch the light.

Exorcising demons and ghosts. I told my closest friend I was forty-one and knew nothing about men and didn't want to wake up at fifty-one and still know nothing, but the truth is much closer to the bone. The truth is that, unable to outrun or contain the contradictions of my life, I had been celibate for the past five years. I had dead-ended into every cold and silent secret I had trailed behind me into a dozen monogamous relationships and scores of one-night stands but never once confronted. Until at last it dawned on me, lying in a bed I had entered only hours ago and would never see again, my hand cradling my chin as I watched the sunlight slowly traversing the coverlet, that all my adult life I had successfully avoided anyone butch enough to turn me on or top me.

And so your question brings me back here, Joan, to things I dream of alone at night, to desires I acknowledge in the dark, to exposed edges and hot, melting shame. To the things about which I neither speak nor write, to the things about which I truly care and therefore make a career of avoiding. "Your writing is very direct," you said. "You're very in-your-face."

I hadn't even known the word *transexual*, nor that it was a word meant for me. In fact, I hadn't even known if transexuals really existed, until at twenty-eight I read Christine Jorgensen's book and finally admitted to being one. A year later, strung out, a suicide note wound in the typewriter and the garden hose snaked out to my shit-green Datsun, I knew I would have surgery or have an end to it. I remember thinking I could always return to this place, but it would be a shame indeed if a liveable life was waiting on the other side of surgery, waiting with a patient, indulgent smile, and I had not lived to see it. So I hauled my weary white ass into the Cleveland Clinic Hospital's Gender Identity Program.

But transexual women were supposed to be straight, and I

had never looked twice at a man, nor felt any erotic heat in their presence. Determined to be a "successful" transexual, I worked earnestly at being straight, at developing the proper attraction to men. I examined their firm little butts, learning to decipher which were cute and which not. I cruised the hair on their chests, their beards, clothing, and stance, the width of their shoulders and the bulge of their cocks, judging its length and thickness by the way it deformed the smooth, muscular profile of whichever jean-clad thigh it rested against. I faithfully reported each foray into heterosexuality to the hospital's noncommittal therapist, desperate to be the good patient upon whom she would confer surgery when my waiting time was up.

I finally informed her that I could not be straight, that I was, in fact, a complete bust with men, that the only thing that still gave me my somewhat limp, estrogen-impaired erections, were other women. I knew then, suicidal as I was and living day-to-day only awaiting surgery, that when they threw me out I might make the trek out to the Datsun after all. "Oh yes," she said, as she peered up from my manila-foldered chart, "we had one of those last year," and she went back to writing case notes in my chart about my "illness." I went back to breathing.

This was pretty amazing stuff at the time. The head of the only other gender program in town had solemnly informed me I could not be a lesbian. "All transexual women," he declared, "want to be penetrated." Well, yes. But I thought maybe he knew even less about woman-to-woman sex than I did, and fearing that his primitive sexual cosmology was accepted as revealed truth within the profession I hoped would save my life, I determined to keep my attraction to women as secret as my own pulse.

I learned, then, that I could be a transexual and attracted to women as well. But could I be a lesbian? Certainly the lesbianism into which I came out in the '70s said I could not. It told me then, as it often does now, that I was a surgically altered male, a man invading women's space, my trespass tolerable to the precise extent I displayed the very oppressive, stereotypically feminine behaviors from which many lesbians were in the most headlong flight. As for what lesbians did in bed, the women's community into which I

emerged reversed the statement of the doctors: "No lesbian," it solemnly intoned, "wants to be penetrated." Penetration, I learned,
was for straight girls.

A transexual she-male freak and a lesbian slut turned on by
penetration in an orifice still under construction was bad enough.
Even worse, I found out that the type of lesbian I wanted meant I
was "into roles." I say I was into roles, Joan, but in truth, it was all in
my head. I learned from every quarter that roles were dead. In-
terred with them went the best of my desires: those strong, femmy
butches who strode arrogantly across my dreams and scared me
half to death with their power and my need.

Perhaps roles *were* dead, though, for in truth I saw neither
femmes nor their butches at the few women's bars or functions I
was allowed to attend. Lesbians who even professed support for
roles were roundly ignored or actively reproached. The lesbianism
into which I came out was dry and pale and bordered by bowl hair-
cuts, no make-up, torn jeans, half-buttoned ubiquitous flannel
shirts, and humorless, hurting women whose sexuality was firmly
suppressed, politically obedient, and completely foreign to my own
erotic tides.

I didn't know butches and femmes still existed, Joan, or even
if they ought to, until you started telling me about them. You taught
me the theory, and even more you taught me respect, resuscitating
the femme parts of me with words like *complex, courageous,
many-layered,* and *specifically lesbian.* "For many years now," you
wrote, "I have been trying to figure out how to explain the special
nature of butch-femme relationships to feminists and lesbian-
feminists who consider butch-femme a reproduction of heterosexual models, and therefore dismiss lesbian communities of the
past and of the present that assert this style."[1]

It was not until sometime later that you taught me the practice as well. And, moreover, that the women I craved still existed,
that it was okay for me to want them, to imagine them. To picture
their hands and cocks and hunger as I lay across my bed, eyes closed
and back arched, rubbing the middle finger of my right hand across
my own recently made clit and pushing the new dildo I'd trimmed

to just the right size and shape deep into my own improbable, impossible cunt.

"Oh, my darling, this play is real," you wrote. "I do long to suck you, to take your courage into my mouth, both cunt, your flesh, and cock, your dream, deep into my mouth, and I do.... She moans, moves, tries to watch, and cannot as the image overpowers her...and then she reaches down and slips the cock into me.... I fall over her.... I am pounding the bed, her arms, anything I can reach. How dare you do this to me, how dare you push me beyond my daily voice, my daily body, my daily fears. I am changing; we are dancing. We have broken through."[2]

And I wondered, Joan, if I would ever break through, as I wandered through one-night stands and short-time lovers, remembered the details of their bodies but not their faces, their technique but not their words. I actively avoided the type of women who excited me, turned aside their gaze, saw them in bars and left. Each time some hidden place inside me burned with a pain I forbade myself to touch or explore, desires and needs well-described by words like *many-layered* and *complex*, but far more distressing and aching than the crisp, black letters on the flat white pages containing them.

The truth is, Joan, I had used sex but could not submit to it. I could come but I could not be present in my body nor use it to express vulnerability or surrender. Sex was something I exchanged for safety or shelter or companionship. Sex was something to attract a lover who wasn't sure if she wanted a transexual, and later sex was something to bind her to me through the shit she would take from friends. And after it was over, sex was a way to be a child again for an hour, maybe two, in safe warm arms.

Sex was a way to humiliate myself and my lovers, to suppress and yet simultaneously revisit again and again those childhood nights when the humiliation was mine and mine alone, when the hot breath on my neck and back belonged to a complete stranger who only looked like my father and whom I met only in the dark. Every time I tried to make love the image of my father hovered above whatever bed I was in like some kind of demented crucifix hung on the wall over our heads. The path I had trodden so long back to my sexuality, my body, and my lesbian self, led in a beeline as long and straight and narrow as the lane-line down a Kansas highway right through to my father.

Incest is a word too ugly and short to do justice to something which is much more than simply ugly and too often not blessedly short. Incest is a daily thing, like the news, like dinner, like brushing your teeth. You can carry it around like a stick of gum in your pocket. It marks your body like a cancerous mole or a burn from hot cooking oil. It colors your thoughts like a drop of ink in a glass of water. It poisons your life like shit down a well.

There are flavors and varieties of incest. There is the straightforward, no-nonsense kind that comes accompanied by clear, sharp snapshot memories developed by Polaroid. These are the ones you can take out and show your friends, who will commiserate; your therapist, who will analyze; and your family, who will deny. They are terrifying, but at least they have defined shapes, colors, and dimensions. Most significantly, at least they are known.

Then there are those as hard to grasp as smoke, the invasions and violations not captured on neat Kodachrome squares, lacking specific memories and penetrations. This is the kind I remember best. Just the glimpse and sense of probing fingers or too-intimate caresses or special glances, and the adult passions of a parent too hot and close and hungry for a needy child to understand. The kind which later in life announces itself with only vague and confusing physical and emotional memories, welling up without warning or reason from unknown and uncharted underground springs, emerging from acts carried out at an age so tender there were no words to frame and recall them. Or perhaps a little older still, when words were at the ready and nearby, but quickly buried so well and far away they have no known latitude or longitude. Although they still manage to wake you from the dark in that familiar sweet sweat with your perpetrator's smell all over them, your child-self screaming with fear and rage like a banshee in the close night air.

And there is another kind of incest, a kind no one even names. This is the transexual kind, and it is a symphony of abuse. It is the

Bach and Beethoven, the Haydn and Mozart of incest. It is orchestrated and complex, with woodwinds and strings, brass notes, and deep bass rhythms. It involves forcing female children to live as boys, withheld hormones and medical treatment, and quick, vicious punishment by those people you love and trust the most for the slightest omission or infraction in dress or behavior. Its terrors and confusions culminate in a second puberty in the full glare of midlife adulthood, followed by a gaudy, baroque crescendo of doctors and scalpels and stitches and blood which, however good the surgery, still leaves you feeling violated and broken inside somehow and never quite sane in your body.

And I am thinking of this, of your words and my life, as I feel his hands on me from behind now, warm and dry, rubbing gently on my buttocks, moving in widening circles until they pause and then dip between my legs, finding and then caressing the pink skin whose origins and construction I still cannot imagine. A single finger pauses at my cunt, stroking just inside my vagina, and then tunnels slowly inward, so slowly in fact that I cannot refrain from pushing back, surprising myself with a soft moan which sounds vaguely ridiculous, even to me. Even to me who has walked the halls of this place many evenings, just listening to the sounds of women caught in the distress of their own lust, their overheated cries and whimpers clutching at my damp insides like a strong hand, or running clean through my body like a knife slicing warm butter.

His finger slides out of my pussy now, and I feel the first taut nudge of his cock. Holding it in his right hand he searches patiently for my open, wondering vagina. After a year of work, my own dance is about to begin, Joan. You have helped to bring me here. I wonder: What will you think reading this? Will you be able to see the lesbian in me, in my experience? Have I come through so many rejections to face another? And if you cannot read this, and read in it other lesbian lives and identities and appetites and passions, then who will? I have heard my own echo in your voice. Will you hear yours in mine?

Our lives become the enactment of those things we can think, the erotic acts and petty daily defiances of the fears haunting the borders of what we will confess to desiring, what we can imagine ourselves wanting to do with our own bodies and those of our lovers. The borders are drawn not by us but by our fears, lines drawn in the sands of our need by rape or shame or abuse, imaginary lines in shifting sands we dare not cross. And standing on the other side of those lines are the women who have gone before, who have stepped past and returned to tell us what lies beyond. They can tell us about the parts of our lives we have lost, whose words we can read but not yet write, whose stories, at once terrifying and exciting, we carry around for years, running them over and over in our minds like old movie reels until at last we recognize them as our own, coming back to us like prodigal children returned in the night or the echoes of our own voices, thrown back at us from a cry of desire uttered so long ago, and in such pain, we neither recall it nor recognize its origins as our own.

He finds my vagina and, gripping my hips, he uses both of his wide hands to pull me back onto his cock. I feel my body parting to take him in, a familiar-strange feeling as he enters me confidently, until at last he is in my flesh up to the hilt. I am struggling to take all of him now, and to stay connected as well: feeling him, testing myself, tightening obscure muscles somewhere far up inside my vagina. He pulls me back, the air forced from my lungs as if someone has struck lightly at my stomach, and just as I catch my breath he begins to move, accelerating now, the apex of his thrusts going off like some liquid explosion deep in the center of my pelvis. I am filled with a kind of wonder, my body showing me things novel and unsuspected.

I close my eyes and collapse into his wife's waiting arms in slow motion. They know it is my first time, and she gently gathers me in, her hands cradling my face, pulling it down and in between her legs. I begin to lick her thighs, her groin, her clit, anything my hungry little mouth can reach, the sweet-smelling hair of her bush containing the sounds now coming from my throat. She laughs, a quick, easy sound, as I raise my hips to take more of her husband's cock inside me. Her plump, buttersmooth hips are tightly encircled, my arms gathering her whole cunt onto my mouth. I suck on it viciously, teething like an infant with bottle while another part of me concentrates on withstanding each delicious withdrawal and fresh, fierce entrance. I am in a kind of heaven, and for the first time in my life I am present in my body and unafraid. I am flying.

"We are the women who like to come, and come hard," Amber Hollibaugh said. "I am a femme, not because I want a man but because I want to feel a butch's weight on my back, feel a butch moving inside my body."[3] Nice as the maleness of my play partner is, it is neither female nor what I want. I begin to play with my head a little, imagining he is a woman and his dick, a dildo strapped on with a soft butch's contradictory, perfectly masculine arrogance. Pleased and emboldened by the effect my imagined lover is having on me, she uses her knees to lever my legs further apart. "Is it okay for you, honey?" she taunts, holding me like that for long seconds, pressing into me, pushing relentlessly forward and down, purposefully using her full weight so I need all my strength to support us both.

She leans far forward over the long muscles of my back, taking her time to pinch each of my nipples, then pausing to wipe the small beads of sweat that have collected at my temples. "What's wrong, baby, is it too much for you?" she purrs. She pulls me backward and enters me so deeply, the O-ring of her strap is suddenly clear and cold on my butt. I catch a glimpse of her over my shoulder, wearing the smile she flashes like a hidden blade, her teeth gleaming in the dim light with pleasure as my face contorts with a faraway look, as if I'd heard the whistle of a train, high-pitched and way off in the distance. Her free hand slips beneath me, trails along my belly, oblivious to my hips jerking sideways, avoiding her, knowing her intent. She searches diligently for my clit, finds it, and begins to worry it, rubbing patiently from side to side with practiced, entirely successful fingers.

I am completely still now, holding my breath to deny her the reward of further response. Until something deep inside me just snaps, bursts clean, and groaning with rage and lust my back arches, a proverbial cat in heat, and she, laughing out loud, answers. Strong, veined hands grip my hips, and she makes the first, killing thrust that begins her final motion, and I know now that she will come fucking me, shouting hoarsely and thrusting into me just as hard as she is able. The warm honey butter-blood begins to flood the cradle of my cunt and I realize that for once, my father is nowhere to be seen. No, nor my fear of masculinity and submission, of penetration and vulnerability, and closing my eyes to surrender to the first delicious tugs of orgasm, I know with a certainty beyond simple trust that I am free.

1. Joan Nestle, "The Femme Question" in *The Persistent Desire: A Femme-Butch Reader,* edited by Joan Nestle (Boston: Alyson, 1992), p. 138.

2. Joan Nestle, "My Woman Poppa," p. 349.

3. See Amber Hollibaugh and Cherríe Moraga, "What We're Rollin' Around in Bed With: Sexual Silences in Feminism" in *Heresies 12: Sex Issue* (1981).

INTERVIEW
WITH A MENACE

TALKING WITH MYSELF: The problem with a book like this, written in a straight-ahead style for a popular audience, is that it leaves so many questions unanswered. Point-counterpoint-counter counterpoint may work for academic texts, but for everyday reading it can get tedious quickly. Yet every front has a back, and every position has a counter, and these are precisely the issues that attract me. To make at least an attempt to address some of the many unanswered questions the text raises for me, I interviewed myself.

Q: FROM THE COVER PHOTO TO THE BIO BLURB, YOU APPEAR TO BE TAKING GREAT PAINS TO POINT OUT WHAT YOU'RE NOT. HOW DO YOU IDENTIFY?

A: I think the interesting thing about your question is that it assumes that I must be anything at all. Maybe I'm intersexed or bisexual or leatherqueer, or all these things together. Maybe for political purposes I'm whoever is unrepresented, whoever is standing alone in the room. The idea that any of us—complex and infinitely faceted as we are—consents to inhabiting identities seems ridiculous to me. My response would be to ask why you need me to produce a sexual or gendered identity. I am just as you see.

Q: ISN'T THAT A BIT PRECIOUS? DON'T YOU NEED AN IDENTITY TO FUNCTION IN SOCIETY?

A: Probably, yes. But that doesn't mean I shouldn't think about it, or that I should consent to it at every turn. Nor do I have to support it or do it to myself. As we talk, what should be apparent is that this is really about power. This isn't about what I am, or how I conceptualize myself, but about your power to require me to have a sex or gender.

Q: YOU MAKE IT SOUND LIKE IDENTITIES ARE ALWAYS INVOLUNTARY IMPOSITIONS.

A: On the contrary, many people choose their identities; others only believe they do. In either case, I certainly defend and respect anyone's right to identify.

But it seems to me that if you're engaged in an activist struggle, you'd better look very closely at the identity you're choosing to mobilize around. Too often we allow ourselves to be defined by our oppression: we become the oppression used against us. Oppress me for my gender, I become "transgender." Then transgender identity becomes one more naturalized category, like male or female. Is that an improvement? And if so, is it the best we can aim for?

Q: DO YOU THINK WE REALLY ESSENTIALIZE IDENTITIES THAT MUCH?

A: Oh yes! Especially sexual identities. One of Foucault's points is that we've privileged sexuality above all else in defining who and what we are. It's the primary way we organize identity in eurocentric cultures.

There's an old joke that illustrates my point. An older man is talking to a young man in a Scottish bar. The old man says, "Look here at the bar. Do ya' see how smooth and just it is? I planed that surface down by me own achin' back. I carved that wood with me own hard labour for eight days. It's a work of art. But do they call me McGreggor-the-Bar-Builder? Nooo...." Then he points out the window. "Eh, Laddy, look out to sea. Do ya' see that pier that stretches out as far as the eye can see? I built that pier with the sweat off me back. I nailed it board by board. There's no better pier in the kingdom. But do they call me McGreggor-the-Pier-Builder? Nooo...." Finally the older man looks around nervously to make sure no one else is paying attention. He leans close to the young man and says, "But ya' fuck *one* goat..."

Q: AREN'T THERE PLENTY OF TRANSPEOPLE WHO LIKE THAT THEY'RE REALLY MEN OR WOMEN, MALE OR FEMALE, AND WHO ARE UNCOMFORTABLE WITH THESE FORAYS AGAINST ESSENTIALIZED IDENTITIES?

A: Yes, to both. But I think it's arguably the case that essentializing has very bad effects for transpeople and generally works to our disadvantage. It places us in the position of pursuing a "realness" defined on other people's bodies. *Real* woman is not just a term defined in my absence; it achieves its utility because of my absence. If I were included in the category, it would be useless.

Claims of realness are usually made at the expense of some other, more marginalized identity appropriated to provide the contrasting not-realness. At Camp Trans there was this interesting split down the middle between post-operative women and those who were pre-operative or non-operative. Those who'd had surgery staunchly maintained that they were real women and ought to be allowed into Michigan because it was the pre-operative women who weren't real. My response was that replacing a policy of "womyn-born womyn only" with "man-made womyn only" wasn't much of an improvement. Needless to say, they were not amused.

What's interesting is how often the tools used against oppressed minorities are simply recycled by them. It's not just that, in Audre Lorde's words, "the master's tools will never dismantle the master's house," but that picking up the master's tools apparently impels us to rebuild the master's house over and over again.

Q: SO YOU'RE NEVER IN FAVOR OF "ONLY" GROUPS—FOR INSTANCE, GROUPS FOR MEN OR WOMEN ONLY?

A: No, but I am against policing the boundaries of such groups and throwing out those you don't think meet the criteria for admission. This recreates hierarchies and legitimacy. In addition, what would you do with those people who don't have a binary sex: Do we exclude all intersexuals by definition? Or should they just resign from the common culture and start their own everything from scratch?

Q: WHAT IF PEOPLE SAY THEY DON'T FEEL SAFE WITH YOU IN THE ROOM?

A: Look, I don't feel safe with me in the room either. Seriously, it's interesting to me that such safety is always secured at the cost of excluding me. I've been kicked out of women's groups in which I was completely silent, meeting after meeting, because someone claimed my very presence made them feel unsafe. I've got news: I'm the last person to deny the reality of gender violence against women, but they need to wake up and smell the coffee. I'm not responsible for anyone else's feelings; what I am responsible for is my own actions. If they feel unsafe, they need to deal with it instead of avoiding the issue and venting on me.

In my experience, I've never seen one of these dynamics occur because of what someone *did*. It's invariably because of what they *are*. You end up being a projection screen for everyone's unfinished business: butches excluded because they were "too male identified"; women body-builders and transmen who started testosterone because they made the space unsafe with their "male energy"; leatherdykes because they were into "violence against women" and that made the vanilla grrlz "feel threatened"; lesbos because the straight women were sure they'd get jumped, and on and on and on. Women's safety—anyone's safety—is a perfectly legitimate concern, but not when it's used to make me the butt of someone else's problems and hostilities.

Q: BY OPENING UP CATEGORIES LIKE "WOMAN," DON'T YOU ALSO

RISK DENYING THE TREMENDOUS OPPRESSION WOMEN SUFFER?

A: I hope not. I think your question mistakes real effects for the fiction of classification. While I have serious reservations about whether it's actually possible to be a woman, it's absolutely true that people so categorized suffer real and profound discrimination, ostracism, and violence. Questioning the reality of the identity is not the same as denying its political effects on those who have occupied it. In fact, if there weren't real oppressions connected with the identity, we wouldn't be talking about it, and essentializing wouldn't have been necessary to begin with. Those real effects are what make it important.

Q: You seem to be suggesting that "the body" as we know it is about meaning, not substance. Doesn't this contradict the fact that we do have real bodies, feel real pain, and so on? Isn't this exactly where most postmodernists lose their audiences—with arguments which seem to ignore the most basic facts of reality?

A: I agree, this is where audiences get lost. But it's not due to faulty concepts as much as faulty communication. Let's use a less loaded example. I once had someone get very upset with me at a seminar, saying: "Look at this book, it's real. It's not just a creation of our 'discourse.'" My response was to ask her to pretend that I was from a preliterate culture and then to tell me all about that book. There was very little she could say, because apart from the fact that it had weight, size, and color, everything about it which gave it its "bookishness" flowed directly from the meanings we attached to it.

In the same way, I'm not denying that we have bodies. That would be silly. But as Thomas Laqueur documents in *Making Sex,* everything we want to say *about* bodies, everything that is culturally resonant for us, already has in it a claim about gender, about similarity or difference.

Q: If that's the case, doesn't it follow that you shouldn't need surgery? Why not do away with surgery and let people

CHANGE MEANINGS INSTEAD?

A: Whenever I hear questions that start with, "But why do you need surgery?" what I hear is an attempt to politicize my body and my choices. It's like saying, "Why not change the meanings around pregnancy so we can do away with abortion?" It's repugnant.

Q: COULDN'T IT JUST BE AN HONEST QUESTION?

A: Honesty is not the issue. It's whose body is on the firing line, and why is it always mine and not yours? For instance, my surgery is supposed to be some kind of "problem" that I have to justify. But I don't want to justify myself, nor do I find myself in need of justification. More to the point, if we stopped politicizing peoples' bodies and meanings, we'd have more surgery, not less, because changing sex or bodies wouldn't be the socially punishing, economically draining, and psychologically debilitating experience it is now.

Q: BUT WHAT ABOUT THE ENORMOUS AMOUNTS OF TIME AND MONEY WHICH GO INTO YOUR PARTICULAR PERFORMANCE OF GENDER? ISN'T THAT SOMETHING TO BE AVOIDED IF POSSIBLE?

A: On the contrary. Other than the surgery, which did cost me several thousands of dollars and a few weeks of downtime from work, I spend almost nothing on my performance of gender. I don't wear any special clothes, act in any particular way, or bother to "correct" people's pronouns, whether they use *Sir* or *Ma'am.*

You, on the other hand, appear to me to be putting lots of effort into your performance of gender. You've worn the "right" suit and tie, you take great care not to cross your legs the "wrong" way. You probably wouldn't be caught dead on the street in a dress and give a wide berth to ladies' lingerie counters. You make sure your voice stays in a low, unmodulated range, buy only men's colognes, lift weights, and would probably freak if some guy addressed you as *Ma'am* or insisted on holding the door for you.

But while you ask after my surgery, you don't ask about the enormous time, effort, and money that goes into your *own* performance of gender, or whether we should be doing away with—not surgery, which affects a minuscule number of people—but the gender system, which affects nearly everyone while consuming millions of hours and dollars for compliance, monitoring, and enforcement.

This is because your gender is "normal." Mine, of course, is queer.

Q: BUT WHY WON'T YOU ANSWER THE DAMN QUESTION?

A: Have you stopped beating your wife?

Q: OKAY. LET'S TRY FROM A DIFFERENT DIRECTION. DON'T YOU THINK THE DEMAND FOR SEX-CHANGE SURGERY WOULD DECREASE IF WE POLICED BODIES LESS?

A: That assumes that decreasing surgery is a good thing, which I think is quite an open question. I do think that if we policed bodies less intensely, more people would seek surgery, not fewer, which would be fine with me since I'd like to see surgery more or less on demand. After all, how many people would have liposuction—or for that matter, hysterectomies or hair transplants—if you were first required to take batteries of psychiatric tests, be diagnosed with a psychiatric condition, submit to twelve months of nonvoluntary therapy, and live in the role for a year full-time? Not to mention losing your job, your spouse, and your kids along the way.

Q: I'M SURE ALL YOUR SALLIES ABOUT NOSE JOBS, A.K.A. "RHINO-IDENTITY DISORDER," GO OVER WELL WITH LIVE AUDIENCES, BUT COULDN'T THAT POTENTIALLY TRIVIALIZE THE PROFOUND PAIN MANY TRANSPEOPLE FEEL ABOUT THEIR BODIES? ISN'T THERE SOMETHING THERE, WHATEVER WE CALL IT?

A: Yes, I think that risk exists. And I should add that I was one of those people, and I had that surgery. You know, with transpeople, as opposed to any other medical intervention, we're forced to construct this entire narrative of legitimacy. To get surgery, you have to mount what I call an Insanity Defense: *I can't help myself, it's something deep inside me, I can't control it.* It's degrading. Getting medical intervention shouldn't require that; it should be a decision between a doctor and her patient. Just like abortion, if you and your personal physician agree that something is medically or psychologically necessary, that should be the end of it.

But back to your point about people's pain. I don't want to trivialize that feeling, which for many of us is both persistent and profound, but rather to look at what kind of cultural practice required me to produce an identity to justify it. Why did my discomfort require justification, and why was the only compelling justification that I had a particular gendered identity? Was my pain or desire insufficient in and of itself so that without the proper paperwork and pedigree I failed to convince? Doesn't the need for a gender identity point instead to our deep and abiding hostility to gender variance? In a civilized society, wanting what you want and getting help should not require you to accept a psychiatric diagnosis, produce a dog-and-pony show of your distress, and provide an identity to justify its realness. That is a debasing and dehumanizing procedure—one with which, I might add, I have lots of first-hand experience.

Critiquing the obligation that we justify ourselves via a gendered identity is not of a piece with denying anyone's distress. Suppose that if we organized primary social identity around occupation, and I became suicidally depressed over wanting to be a doctor but couldn't become one, I have no doubt that psychiatry would respond to my consequent psycho-social dislocation by inaugurating an Occupational Identity Disorder, complete with etiology, prognosis, pathogenesis, and treatment for my "condition."

Q: THAT DODGES THE CENTRAL FACT THAT SOMEONE CUTS OFF HER PENIS.

A: I think that's a very interesting formulation. Someone even used the argument that "it's a pathology if I cut off all the fingers on my right hand." No one ever references the reverse formulation—of a transexual male wanting to grow a penis—because it's assumed that everyone would love to have the magic cock. That's regarded as power, and desire for it is normal.

Correspondingly, transexual woman are unerringly described as "cutting off their dicks." No one ever formulates this act as gaining a cunt—not even lesbians, feminists, or transgender women. A cunt in Western culture is reducible to the vagina: the place for penetration by penises. A vagina is a hole, nothing—lack, emptiness, and absence—and nobody needs nothing. My friend Jeanine Cogan of the American Psychiatric Association points out this inherent sexism, not to mention phallo-centrism, in the way intercourse is always understood through terms of penetration rather than engulfment. In *Everything You Always Wanted to Know About Sex (But Were Afraid to Ask)*, David Reuben explains the "failure" of lesbianism by pointing out that zero plus zero still equals zero. That's as fine a formulation of Western thought as I've seen.

Q: EVEN ACCEPTING THAT ARGUMENT, TRANSEXUALITY SEEMS DIFFERENT IN THAT IT'S NOT ONLY ABOUT GAINING SOMETHING, AS YOU POINT OUT, BUT ABOUT HATING YOUR BODY.

A: First, all of us don't hate our bodies. Second, my body didn't come this way—I made it this way. I like it this way. I'm angry at the parade of right-wing feminists and pseudoqueers who want to sit in judgment of my life and what I do with my body. Get a life, and while you're at it, stop trying to appropriate and colonize mine.

Finally, lots of people dislike their bodies, or fervently wish they were different. Such feelings probably date back to the small chimp wishing he could beat up the alpha male chimp. The desire of people to change their bodies is as old as humankind. Some are differently abled, some are unhappily fat, some are differently colored, and some are differently gendered. Look, if my mom hates her wrinkles and gets an age-lift—face, boobs, lipo, the works—and is as happy as the proverbial clam feeling young again, no one is going to say she's crazy. But if I want a cunt, even lesbians think I must be some kind of mental case. You figure it out.

Q: WITH ALL THAT SAID ABOUT DECONSTRUCTING BODIES AND IDENTITIES, WHY WEAR A T-SHIRT THAT READS TRANSEXUAL MENACE?

Doesn't that contradict everything you've been saying about de-essentializing identities?

A: First of all, you don't have to be transexual to be a Menace. Anyone can be a member. It's more of a dis-organization than anything else. And yes, I wear the T-shirt. Not to occupy the identity but to contest it: to subvert the idea that whatever it stands for is shameful, and to reverse the erasure of genderqueerness from our communal discourse. But I have no intention of being a transexual or transgender person. I've also proudly worn other T-shirts—from Lesbian Avengers and Hermaphrodites With Attitude, to name a few. These are tactics, not identities.

Q: You seem to want to have your cake and eat it too. You want us to see "truths" about the body as culturally constructed and untrue, at the same time that you want an exemption for your own ideas—which you want us to believe really are true.

A: Not at all. Culturally constructed does not equal untrue, as if there was some neutral place, outside of culture or language, from which truthful statements can be made. The point is not to separate truth from untruth—like the Dead from the Undead—and drive a stake through the heart of the bad one. All truths are cultural and have political implications, including mine.

Q: Very clever, but when you cut to the chase doesn't it mean that, just like everyone else, you're pursuing your own political agenda?

A: Yes. And people should take into account that everything I've been saying has an explicit political agenda to it: I am absolutely trying to use language and knowledge to subvert certain ideas about bodies, gender, and desire.

I'm doing a little second-order subversion, that's all. Instead of claiming a new set of things about bodies, I'm merely saying nasty things about what has already been said. But I'm not interested in being the New Boss who gets to lay down the law of how all bodies must be.

Q: Doesn't this confuse your audiences?

A: Is confusion a bad thing? Maybe the price of admission to finding a less oppressive vision and disturbing our certainty about gender is enduring a little confusion. Maybe that's a sign of progress rather than failure.

Thinking in language is challenging enough for most of us. But this is thinking *about* thinking—second-order stuff—and it's really tough. Like chasing your own tail.

People often complain to me that they like the ideas but aren't quite sure what my point is. We're so accustomed to people pushing an agenda of truth-claims that when someone doesn't do it, it's very disconcerting. We want to weigh one claim against the other, sort out the small points, debate pros and cons. We want something to be wrong and to believe in something firm and unshakeable and right. An argument about arguments is unsettling.

I love something Foucault said, with which I continue to struggle: "Prefer what is positive and multiple: difference over uniformity, flows over unities.... Believe that what is productive is not sedentary but nomadic."

I get a lot of folks who look at the idea of there being few objective truths and then are completely aghast at this canyon of irrationality opening at their feet. Without an anchor to reality they feel like they're spinning off into space. But for others—if you survive the initial vertigo—that's a definition of freedom.

Q: Doesn't undermining identity constitute a political attack on feminism's "Radical Right," writers like Mary Daly and Andrea Dworkin, who stake their case on a naturalized womanhood that is inherently nurturing, nonviolent, cooperative, and so on?

A: I would be disappointed if they read it in any other way. Their attempts to install an essentialized "woman" who has some kind of proto-woman's experience (which usually looks suspiciously middle-class, white, urban, and American) is an attack on the legitimacy, bodies, and political identities of all the other women trapped outside their neat boundaries: stone butches, women of color, transgender women, Third World women, passing women, dyke daddies, hermaphrodite women, androgen-insensitive women, drag kings, leatherdykes, steroid-shooting body-builders, faggot-identified dykes, and on and on.

But now we've come full circle again. These discussions are not about the reality of identities, but the reality of power: whose womanhood counts, who is relegated to being the gendertrash, and who gets to act as judge. I don't think my explanation is any more "right" than theirs. I think both of us have explicit political agendas and make arguments in their service. Which one should you choose? The one that works for you. As the woman at the carnival says: At some point you pays your money and you makes your choice.

Q: SO HOW DO YOU HANDLE IT WHEN YOU'RE INVITED TO SPEAK AT SOME GIG "AS A TRANSEXUAL," OR "AS A TRANSGENDER ACTIVIST"?

A: I accept, of course. But since I've never been comfortable with the labels, the first thing out of my mouth is that, while I'm grateful to be invited, I don't consider myself either one. I hope I'm there for what I have to say, not for what I am perceived to be.

In these times of rampant political correctness, panels are always supposed to be one of each, as if all good thinking were conducted in the halls of Baskin-Robbins University with the mandatory presence of each of the thirty-one flavors.

Q: ISN'T THAT ALSO A RESULT OF PEOPLE'S DESIRE TO BE INCLUSIVE?

A: Yes, it is, and I recognize that sometimes it's too easy for me to poke fun at such practices. U.S. politics are so screwed up that if you don't consider diversity in the identities you invite, your panels end up basically white, male, and middle class. One benefit of identity lists is that they do make you look for what kinds of people aren't represented.

Q: At last something positive!

A. What it usually boils down to is whose needs count and who is considered disposable. And babe, I'm sure you can imagine where the priorities of genderqueers fit in.

Q: Which brings us to the issue of organizations. You're the Executive Director of the Gender Public Advocacy Coalition, GenderPAC. Isn't that a transgender group?

A: I hope not. I've said from the very beginning that I have no interest in heading another round of identity politics. While it is true that GenderPAC came out of the gender community, it's also true that we look at any issue connected with gender-based oppression. The motto on every piece of letterhead is "gender, affectional, and racial equality."

Q: Which means what, exactly, in practice?

A: We do a number of things. We're like a small amalgam of the Human Rights Campaign, Lambda Legal Defense Fund, Gay and Lesbian Alliance Against Defamation, and the National Gay and Lesbian Task Force. We do regular educational lobbying on Capitol Hill, plus facilitate an open National Gender Lobbying Day every year or so. We provide an online and printed news service for gender activism called *InYourFace!* We do public relations to place gender-positive stories in the media while undertaking antidefamation work around transphobic pieces. We fund street activism. We conduct community-based research into things like hate crimes and employment discrimination. We try to help genderqueer prisoners wherever there's a case having national or regional implications. And, although we can't yet afford to litigate cases, we try to file amicus briefs where there is a chance to set legal precedent.

Q: Don't you risk collapsing together several different kinds of oppression?

A: Yes, I think that's one of risks we run. There's no intention or belief that these are all interchangeable. It *is* my conviction that people inhabit complex, messy, multilayered lives, and any movement failing to make these kinds of connections runs the larger risk of being morally bankrupt. When the EMS technician backed away from Tyra Hunter, bleeding on the street after a hit-and-run, and the ambulance took twenty minutes to get to the scene (in the ghetto) in the first place, was that incident about gender, race, or class—or all three?

Q: SO WHAT DO YOU HOPE YOUR AUDIENCE COMES AWAY FROM ALL THIS WITH?

A: I don't want an audience. I want a movement.

Q: MEANING?

A: Meaning that although many of our older liberal movements grew as institutional powers, they appear largely spent as philosophical forces. Feminism has been fundamentally unable to grapple effectively with homosexuality, and it certainly has no response to genderqueers. Gay liberation goes from strength to strength in national politics—which is wonderful—but seems to have less and less new to say.

If even such "hard" categories as gender, race, sex, and orientation are not *causes* of our oppression but its *effects*, then we need a new kind of political struggle, one that seeks not just to overthrow the oppression, but the categories as well. For if identities are themselves products of oppression, requiring us to balkanize the complexity of our lives into so many different parcels—race, class, feminism, gay rights, transgender—then the familiar liberal project of separate-but-equal movements no longer makes sense.

We need a new political movement that takes the complexities of our lived experience as its starting point, one that mobilizes it as a strength to be used and not a weakness to be avoided; that encourages us to build on the many layers of that experience rather than separating them further; one that bids us to make connections rather than sever them. For the truth is that we are whole people, and not just so many separate constituencies walking around inside a common and convenient package. Our lives and what we have suffered are not the stumbling blocks to our freedom but the keys to obtaining it. We need a movement that takes this both as its primary method and its common political goal.

Will a movement without identities be messy? Yes, as messy and multilayered as we actually are. Won't a political movement lacking a unified subject have contradictions and discord? Of course. But as Judith Butler suggested, maybe it's time to stop sacrificing the complexity of our lives at the altar of unified identity, to acknowledge our contradictions and take political action with all of them intact. Unity is a product of encouraging diversity, not of reenforcing its absence.

Our contradictions and differences are more than political obstacles: they are reminders of our boundlessness, confirmations that we can never be fully captured or circumscribed, that no label or movement can ever hope to encompass all we are or hope to be. And that diversity is our strength in the face of the familiar, tyrannical Western project to impose the monolithic, all-enveloping truths that marginalized, suppressed, and erased us in the first place.

I think Marjorie Garber is right in pointing out that we are experiencing a failure of the categories. There is room here, I believe, for a third force, another kind of politics, and people who move from the sidelines and get involved now have a shot at making a real difference.

I don't know whether that will happen, but it's what I'm giving my life to at this point. We need an inclusive movement that is committed to making connections across the boundaries for our common good. Maybe if we're willing to extend our hands over the walls we've erected, together we can do what we could not do separately.

But for that we need to trust each other, we need to refuse to marginalize our own minorities.

If we've learned anything from human history, it's that people can endure suffering when they believe it's meaningful. And the truth is, most of us experience suffering and look for ways to give it meaning, to use what we've learned and what we've experienced to make the world a better place for our passing. But we don't know how, so we go through the motions, wondering if that's all there is.

I'll close with a remembrance from *Lawrence of Arabia*. Lawrence (Peter O'Toole) is involved with the Arabs in a revolt against the Turks during World War I. The Arab tribesmen must take the Port of Aqaba to secure the Arabian Peninsula. Aqaba is protected on the seaward side by an enormous cannon that can sink a fleet of ships, and on the landward side by the Nefud desert. Aqaba cannot be taken, but it must.

Lawrence declares to Sharif Ali (Omar Sharif), "I'm going to take Aqaba from the landward side."

"The Nefud is the worst place God ever created," says Ali.

"I'm going to take it with fifty men."

"Fifty men cannot take Aqaba."

"If fifty men walked out of the Nefud, are they not fifty men others might follow?"

"Yes," admits Ali, "but the Nefud cannot be crossed."

"Come here," Lawrence says, pointing into the distance. "Aqaba is over there...it's just a matter of going."

Over the next couple of years, with God's help, fifty or a hundred of us will step out of this political desert together. And when we do, we will be fifty whom others might follow. A unified national movement to end gender-based oppression is right before us...it's just a matter of going.

A SELECTED CHRONOLOGY OF THE TRANSEXUAL MENACE AND GENDERPAC

1993

TransWomen Contest MWMF's Exclusion Policy

[Hart, MI: 14 August 93] Six trans-identified women and friends are evicted from the Michigan Womyn's Music Festival. They set up camp across from the main gates of the festival in a public forest. They are pleasantly surprised when scores of festival attendees leave the festival grounds to attend several workshops they offer on trans-inclusion and lesbian/feminism. Four transgender women quietly re-enter the festival to contest the exclusionary policy, but are again evicted by festival owners.

All stories courtesy of *InYourFace!*, the news-only service for gender activism. You can subscribe to *InYourFace!* or view past issues at the GenderPac web site, www.gpac.org. The printed version is published twice annually and is available free by becoming a member of GenderPAC. Membership inquiries only can be directed to GenderPAC, Attn: Dana Priesing, 733 Fifteenth Street NW, 7th Floor, Washington, DC 20005.

FALLS CITY TRANSEXUAL MAN ASSAULTED AND RAPED ON CHRISTMAS DAY

[Falls City, NB: 25 December 93] John Lotter and Thomas Nissan take turns raping local transexual man Brandon Teena after beating him, because they are infuriated with his living as a male. They force him to shower afterward to remove the evidence, and then threaten to kill him if he reports the incident. When a bloody and visibly traumatized Brandon attempts to swear out a complaint, Sheriff Charles Laux ignores his charges, but harasses him on his male appearance.

TRIPLE MURDER IN NEBRASKA FARMHOUSE

[Falls City, NB: 27 December 93] Fulfilling a threat made on Christmas Day, John Lotter and Thomas Nissan break in on Brandon Teena at a rented Nebraska farmhouse and murder him and two friends, execution-style, as they sleep. According to Nissan's later testimony, Brandon is first stabbed in the stomach with a knife and, when he lies moaning but still alive, he is killed when Lotter steps forward and shoots him in the head.

1994

STONEWALL 25 PROTEST

[New York, NY: 20 March 94] Reminding everyone that it was drag and transpeople like Sylvia Rivera, Marsha P. Johnson, and Yvonne P. Ritter who ignited the Stonewall Rebellion twenty-five years ago in 1969, a new group, Transexual Menace, joins with It's Time America!, Transgender Nation, and the Transgender Law Conference to protest Stonewall 25's continued exclusion of *transgender* from the title of their Gay, Lesbian, and Bisexual event.

CAMP TRANS FUNDRAISER HELD

[New York, NY: 7 June 94] Almost a thousand dollars is donated at the "Unity & Inclusion" fundraiser for Camp Trans organized by the Transexual Menace at New York's Lesbian and Gay Community Center. Speakers include Kate Bornstein, Holly Hughes, Leslie Feinberg, Amber Hollibaugh, Cheryl Clarke, Minnie Bruce Pratt, and representatives from the Lesbian Avengers.

CAMP TRANS DRAWS HUNDREDS FROM MWMF

[Hart, MI: 13 August 94] The second Camp Trans, the educational event scheduled to coincide with the MWMF, is held in the woods across from the festival's main gates.

CONTROVERSY FLARES OVER GAY GAMES

[New York, NY: 14 June 94] Menace members leaflet the Gay Games '94 over their policy of requiring transwomen to document why they should be allowed to compete as women. In a turnaround, the Gay Games board agrees to publicly rescind the policy; however, the anticipated horde of trans-UberWomen sweeping the women's events fails to materialize.

VILLAGE VOICE PICKETED OVER BRANDON TEENA COVERAGE

[New York, NY: 18 April 94] The Menace pickets outside the offices of the *Village Voice*, protesting a salacious portrayal of murdered transexual man Brandon Teena as a confused but sexually active butch.

TRANSEXUAL MENACE CONFRONTS JANICE RAYMOND

[New York, NY: November 94] Janice Raymond speaks at Judith's Room, NYC's feminist bookstore. Her book, *The Transsexual Empire: The Making of a She-Male*, alleges that transpeople are designed expressly by deranged surgeons to invade women's space. She is met by two dozen pissed-off she-males, designed expressly by deranged Menace surgeons to invade women's bookstores.

1995

LSM CONTROVERSY ON TRANSINCLUSION

[New York, NY: 1995] Two members of the Menace try to join LSM, a local lesbian/feminist S/M support group, and are told that they must be post-operative. Both immediately declare themselves pre-operative and promise to leaflet all future LSM events until the policy is lifted. After a year of dialogue and private diplomacy, LSM members vote to change the policy.

BRANDON TEENA MURDER TRIAL VIGIL HELD

[Falls City, NB: 15 May 95] Forty gender activists from across the nation attend a peaceful memorial vigil outside the murder trial of Brandon Teena at the Falls City courthouse. By lunch, local neo-Nazis are circling the block, spitting at attendees and giving "Sieg Heil" salutes. At a memorial service the previous day, Kate Bornstein, Leslie Feinberg, Minnie Bruce Pratt, and Aphrodite Jones speak.

DEBBIE FORTE MURDERED

[Haverhill, MA: 15 May 95] As activists are leaving the Brandon Teena murder trial in Nebraska, Debbie Forte is savagely murdered by Michael J. Thompson in Haverhill, Massachusetts. She suffers three stab wounds to the chest, multiple slash wounds, a smashed nose, blows to the head and face, and signs of strangulation. Thompson confesses to a coworker that he killed her after they began "messing around" and he discovered she had a penis.

GENDER PUBLIC ADVOCACY COALITION FOUNDED

[Cincinnati, OH: 10 June 95] The Gender Public Advocacy Coalition (GenderPAC) is informally launched at a large gender conference, "The Be-All," held in the Midwest, and funded with gifts from a handful of donors intent on supporting the growing trend toward national gender activism.

HRCF TARGET OF NATIONAL PROTEST OVER ENDA

[New York, NY: 19 June 95] Gender organizations call for widespread protests of the Human Rights Campaign Fund (HRCF) when it again introduces an Employment Non-Discrimination Bill (ENDA) which protects sexual orientation but not gender expression. The Transexual Menace, now grown to forty chapters, attempts its first sustained, nationally coordinated campaign and leaflets HRCF fundraisers in sixteen cities, including New Orleans, Cincinnati, Philadelphia, San Antonio, Cleveland, San Francisco, Boston, New York, Houston, Atlanta, and Chicago.

MENACE PUSHES FOR TRANSINCLUSION IN NOW

[Columbus, OH: 18 July 95] After a resolution recognizing transpeople as part of feminism is unanimously passed by New Jersey NOW, a dozen transactivists circulate a petition bearing the resolution at NOW's yearly National Conference. One of the first of over three hundred signatories is NOW's first president, Ms. Eleanor Smeal. Although only two out of over a hundred voting representatives are opposed, the resolution is tabled and languishes for the next two years.

EMS TECHNICIAN CEASES TREATING DYING TRANSWOMAN

[Washington, DC: 7 August 95] After Tyra Hunter is critically injured in a hit-and-run in Washington, DC, an EMS technician administering first-aid cuts open her pants to discover she has a penis. He then stops treating her and begins making jokes about the prostrate woman to a horrified crowd. Ms. Hunter dies of her injuries and the DC Fire Department refuses to investigate the incident, release the technician's name, or acknowledge a problem despite intense efforts by local activists and statements from eight eyewitnesses. Over two thousand people attend Tyra's funeral.

HRCF & GENDER ACTIVISTS REACH AGREEMENT, PROTESTS END

[Washington, DC: 18 September 95] The Human Rights Campaign

Fund (HRCF) flies leaders of seven transgender groups to Washington for a marathon four-hour meeting in which a series of agreements is struck. HRCF issues a statement agreeing to work collaboratively on issues such as hate crimes, and "...to assist transgender representatives with an amendment strategy in the context of ENDA," adding, "both groups will work in good faith to continue dialogue and to build coalition in the context of ending violence and discrimination against this community." The agreement effectively ends the nationwide protests of HRCF over their Employment Non-Discrimination Bill (ENDA), which would protect sexual orientation but not gender expression.

1ST NATIONAL GENDER LOBBY DAY HELD IN DC

[Washington, DC: 4 October 95] Building on work by the Transgender Law Conference and It's Time America!, GenderPAC hosts the first National Gender Lobby Day in Washington, DC. Over a hundred activists show up on October 4 for two days of intensive lobbying on hate crimes, employment discrimination, and other issues. The sight of scores of transexuals, crossdressers, transgenders, their friends and supporters in the Rayburn Building cafeteria transfixes congressional aides. We control your horizontal; we control your vertical; we control your hormones.

MENACE PICKETS DC MAYOR, DEMANDS JUSTICE FOR TYRA HUNTER

[Washington, DC: 6 October 95] Three dozen Menace activists loudly picket the City Hall offices of Mayor Marion Barry, demanding an end to the cover-up surrounding Ms. Hunter's treatment by the EMS. He meets with protesters briefly, but only agrees to arrange a meeting between them and Fire Chief Otis Latin to discuss the matter.

SEAN O'NEILL CHARGED WITH RAPE ASSAULT

[Colorado Springs, CO: 1995] Nineteen-year-old transgender man Sean O'Neill is charged with sexual assault and statutory rape for having consensual sexual contact with two other teenagers, one of them underage. The girl's parents are outraged when they discover that Sean has female genitals and thus is "really" a lesbian. Although Sean is slight of build and just over five feet tall, the District Attorney labels him a dangerous and predatory "pedophile," stacking charges so that O'Neill faces forty years in the state prison. On advice of his attorney, Sean pleads guilty to a single count.

DC FIRE DEPARTMENT OPENS INVESTIGATION

[Washington, DC: 6 December 95] In the face of continuing pressure from the queer community, the DC Fire Department reluctantly opens an investigation into the EMS's treatment of Tyra Hunter.

1996

ABC'S 20/20 AIRS SEGMENT ON TRANSACTIVISM

[New York, NY: 19 January 96] ABC airs a twelve-minute segment on TOPS (Transgender Officers Protect & Serve), the country's first organization for transgender peace officers, National Gender Lobby Day, and the rise of gender activism. Despite a sympathetic producer, on-air interviewer John Stossel verbally humiliates one of the TOPS officers on national TV over how she looks in a dress. The Menace pickets ABC's NY offices the following morning.

DEMONSTRATION AT SEAN O'NEILL SENTENCING

[Colorado Springs, CO: 6 February 96] Protesters fly in from across the country to demonstrate quietly outside the Colorado Springs courthouse where Sean O'Neill is to be sentenced. Later the same day they pack the courtroom for his hearing, and two of them, Jamison Green and Deputy Sheriff Tonye Barreto-Neto, testify in open court on Sean's behalf. In what is considered a victory for the defense, Sean is sentenced to only ninety days in the county jail. His elated public defender dons a Menace T-shirt and accompanies protesters to a local watering hole to celebrate.

JOHN LOTTER SENTENCED TO DEATH FOR MURDER OF BRANDON TEENA

[Falls City, NB: 22 February 96] A judge sentences John Lotter to death for the triple murders of transman Brandon Teena and two of his friends. His accomplice, Tom Nissan, who testified against Lotter, is sentenced to life in prison. The announcement of the death sentence prompts *Saturday Night Live*'s Norm MacDonald to make fun of the murders on *SNL*'s "Weekend Update" segment, saying, "I think everyone in the story deserved to die." Protests are filed by GenderPAC and GLAAD with NBC, and assurances are issued by NBC's Office of Standards and Practices that *SNL* has been "sensitized."

HRCF'S ELIZABETH BIRCH TESTIFIES FOR TRANSINCLUSION IN HATE CRIMES BILL

[Washington, DC: 22 March 96] Testifying for the re-authorization of the Hate Crimes Statistics Act now working its way through Congress, Elizabeth Birch, Executive Director of the Human Rights Campaign Fund, fulfills a pledge she made during sometimes-heated exchanges with transcommunity leaders last year to support inclusion of gender in national hate crimes legislation.

GLMA CLARIFIES MISSION, REMOVES TRANSPEOPLE

[San Francisco, CA: 5 April 96] In an unannounced and unpublicized move, the board of the Gay and Lesbian Medical Association (GLMA) elects to "clarify" its mission statement in May by removing transpeople from its mission statement and letterhead. Canadians are also removed. An outcry ensues. In completely gratuitous remarks, a Menace spokestrans declares, "We are shocked, shocked! at this blatant display of Canada-phobia—it is simply inexcusable that anyone would want to treat our neighbors to the north in this thoughtless and cavalier manner."

CHRISTIAN PAIGE BRUTALLY MURDERED, KILLER AT LARGE

[Chicago, IL: 11 April 96] A twenty-four-year-old transsexual woman and well-known performer, Christian Paige, is found murdered. She has been brutally beaten about the head, strangled, and then stabbed over a dozen times; the murder scene was then set afire. Her body is discovered by firefighters when they enter to put out the fire.

GLMA RECLARIFIES MISSION, REINSTATES TRANSPEOPLE

[San Francisco, CA: 2 May 96] After dozens of activists, led by MD Joy Schaeffer, picket a GLMA meeting, the board belatedly votes to reinstate transpeople in its mission statement and letterhead. Canadians are not reinstated. Canadian-born news anchor Peter Jennings ignores the item during the ABC *Evening News,* but veteran network watchers note that he appears visibly shaken by the day's events.

TOP PSYCHIATRISTS' CONFERENCE PICKETED

[New York, NY: 5 May 96] Activists from Transexual Menace, ACT-UP, and TOPS demonstrate outside the American Psychiatric Association's national conference in New York City, protesting the use of the diagnosis of Gender Identity Disorder (GID) to stigmatize "pre-homosexual" or gender-variant children as well as transgender adults seeking surgery.

CHRISTIAN PAIGE VIGIL HELD

[Chicago, IL: 27 May 96] Transactivists and friends hold a quiet demonstration/vigil in Chicago's Daly Center to focus public awareness on the life and murder of Christian Paige. Some carry placards reading *Transpeople are NOT disposable people.*

THREE WOMEN SHOT BY TORONTO SERIAL KILLER

[Toronto, ON: 23 May 96] On the evening of Canada's 4th of July (Victoria Day), a serial killer stalks and shoots three sex workers, all believed to be transgendered. Although it later emerges that one of the victims was a nontransexual woman, the Toronto police department autopsy reveals that all three victims were forced to kneel and face their assailant, apparently so he could make some sort of statement before shooting each of them in the head. Local activists stage a memorial march. The killer is apprehended only weeks later. He is a quiet and otherwise unremarkable married father of two.

NATIONAL SURVEY OF TRANSVIOLENCE LAUNCHED

[New York, NY: 5 June 96] Responding to complaints by Congressional legislative assistants that there is no evidence of transviolence, GenderPAC officially launches its first National Survey of Transviolence to document the problem. Support is provided by the New York office of the Gay and Lesbian Antiviolence Project (AVP).

HATE CRIMES BILL OMITS TRANSVIOLENCE AGAIN

[Washington, DC: 4 July 96] President Clinton signs the Hate Crimes Statistics Act (HCSA) passed by Congress, which reauthorizes continued tracking of bias-related crimes. Despite the tide of transmurders and supportive testimony by the HRCF's Elizabeth Birch, hate crimes based on gender are still excluded.

NEW YORK TIMES RECOGNIZES GENDER ACTIVISM

[New York, NY: 8 September 96] In a groundbreaking story, the *New York Times* prints a piece on the front page of the "Nation" section of its Sunday edition detailing the emerging face of gender activism. Entitled "They Fight for Respect," the article covers the Deborah Forte Memorial Vigil, the emergence of the gender movement, the Transexual Menace and GenderPAC, and the 1st National Gender Lobby Day.

FORTE KILLER PLEADS GUILTY, GETS LIFE

[Cambridge, MA: 16 September 96] Michael Thompson is sentenced to life in prison after pleading guilty to the murder of Debbie Forte. A dozen members of Transexual Menace and GenderPAC gather outside the courthouse in a quiet memorial vigil. Members of Debbie's family stop by to thank demonstrators for their support.

VERMONT RALLIES FOR CROSSDRESSING TEEN

[Burlington, VT: 5 October 96]   Dozens of local supporters and members of the Transexual Menace gather in downtown Burlington to voice support and concern for suspended crossdressing teen, Matthew Stickney. Stickney, who identifies variously as gay, drag, and crossdressing, was suspended from Burlington high school on September 9 after wearing a dress to class. He was verbally harassed by classmates, then accused by the principal of creating a disturbance and ordered to change his attire.

APA PICKETED OVER GID, MEETS WITH PROTESTERS

[Chicago, IL: 19 October 96] Forty-eight demonstrators from Transexual Menace, It's Time America!, Queer Nation, the Lesbian Avengers, TOPS, various leatherboys, and at least one intersexed person picket for Gender Identity Disorder (GID) reform outside the American Psychiatric Association's (APA) national conference for hospital administrators. APA representatives hold an hour-long meeting with demonstrators to discuss their concerns.

HERMAPHRODITES WITH ATTITUDE PICKET PEDIATRICIANS

[Boston, MA: 26 October 96] In the first public demonstration by intersexuals in modern history, twenty-six gender activists from Hermaphrodites With Attitude and Transexual Menace gather outside the annual meeting of the American Academy of Pediatricians (AAP) to protest AAP's continued support of Intersex Genital Mutilation (IGM). The AAP releases a press statement declaring that IGM is in the child's best interests, since it prevents possible future psychological and social trauma.

MENACE PROTESTS ACCUSED PRISONER RAPIST

[Lindenhurst, NY: 28 October 96] As the issue of prisoner rape continues to be ignored by both queer and feminist organizations, a small group of Menace activists leaflets this quiet Long Island town protesting the alleged rapes of openly gay inmate, Maurice

Mathie, over a six-year period by the sergeant in charge of security at the Suffolk County Jail.

GENDERPAC FORMALIZED

[King of Prussia, PA: 2 November 96] Twelve national organizations from across the transcommunity sign Articles of Association for GenderPAC and form a board of directors. The signing marks the first time the gender community has consolidated its resources to address gender-based oppression. In a move to rapidly diversify the board, BiNet USA, the National Center for Lesbian Rights, and NGLTF are all invited to join. They accept.

APA OFFICES PICKETED IN DC, BROAD COALITION SUPPORTS CHANGE

[Washington, DC: 8 November 96] A broad coalition of national groups, including the Menace, the National Gay and Lesbian Task Force (NGLTF), BiNet USA, the National Center for Lesbian Rights (NCLR), and the International Gay and Lesbian Human Rights Commission (IGLHRC), holds a joint protest outside the national offices of the American Psychiatric Association during NGLTF's "Creating Change" conference, marking the first time major queer groups have joined together around the issue of Gender Identity Disorder (GID) reform.

CHANELLE PICKETT MURDERED

[Cambridge, MA: 20 November 96] Chanelle Pickett, one of two transexual twin sisters, is murdered after she goes home with a date for the evening. The man turns himself in to police, claiming he panicked after finding out Ms. Pickett had a penis. The District Attorney at first credits his story, until several local transexual women testify that he was well-known at local gender bars and specifically sought out pre-operative women on numerous occasions.

NGLTF CALLS FOR GID REFORM, OTHER QUEER GROUPS FOLLOW

[Washington, DC: 12 December 96] Kerry Lobel, Executive Director of the National Gay and Lesbian Task Force (NGLTF), issues a statement to Dr. Harold Eist, President of the American Psychiatric Association (APA), urging that the diagnosis of Gender Identity Disorder (GID) be eliminated as a diagnosable disorder in children and be replaced with a nonstigmatizing physical condition in adults. Lobel's statement is especially noteworthy since it was NGLTF who persuaded the APA to remove homosexuality as a disorder twenty-six years ago. The statement, which requests a meeting with the APA to discuss the issue, is quickly followed by letters from the National Center for Lesbian Rights and GenderPAC.

CHANELLE PICKETT MEMORIAL SERVICE HELD

[Cambridge, MA: 22 December, 96] Hundreds of gay, lesbian, bisexual, and transgender members of the local community gather in a local church to remember slain transgender woman, Chanelle Pickett. After her surviving twin, Gabrielle, addresses the crowded church and lights several candles to her slain sister's memory, the assembly marches to the nearby State House to lay a memorial wreath.

1997

TRIAL BEGINS ON TRANSPRISONER RAPE

[Madison, WI: 20 January 97] The jury trial of raped trans-inmate Dee Farmer, whose case went all the way up to the Supreme Court, begins January 21 in Madison, Wisconsin. After Farmer was raped in prison, she charged that prison authorities knew of her transgender status but failed to take steps to protect her from inevitable sexual assault. Wisconsin Federal Court Judge John Shabaz threw out Ms. Farmer's case, finding that prison officials had not been properly notified that she faced a special risk. Ms. Farmer, with no money and few resources, appealed her case all the way to the U.S. Supreme Court, which last year upheld her right to sue.

GenderPAC, Bi-Net USA, & HRCF Lobby Together on the Hill

[Washington, DC: 14 January 97] Today marks the turning of a corner as—for the first time—the Human Rights Campaign Fund (HRCF), Bi-Net USA, and GenderPAC make a series of joint calls on Capitol Hill to conduct basic education around bi/herm/trans issues and discuss the prospects for trans-inclusion in the Employment Non-Discrimination Bill (ENDA) with some of the bill's sponsors. The day's activities are organized by HRCF's Senior Policy Advocate, Nancy Buermeyer.

Coalition for Sexual Freedom Begins

[New York, NY: 10 January 97] The National Coalition for Sexual Freedom (NCSF) announces its formation and begins to form a board. Although it originates in the leather community, NCSF leaders quickly adopt an inclusive mission statement focusing on national advocacy for issues relating to "sexual orientation, identity, or desire." They will address age of consent, anti-sodomy, child custody, and other laws that discriminate against alternative sexual or affectional practice. Founding member Susan Wright approaches GenderPAC about joining.

Chicago Intersexual Dies as Result of Alleged Police Brutality

[Hoffman Estates, IL: 16 January, 97] The family of Logan Smith, twenty-three, files a wrongful death suit against the Hoffman Estates police. Smith had been in a car the police had stopped for a minor traffic violation. In the ensuing altercation, Smith, an intersexed person born with an external bladder, is allegedly kicked in the stomach by the arresting officers. Once in police custody, Smith's repeated complaints of severe abdominal pain are ignored and he dies shortly after of septic infection.

Another TG Prisoner Alleges Prison Rape

[Walla Walla, WA: 25 January 97] Crystal Marie Schwenk, a transexual inmate in the Washington state prison system, files a civil rights action against a prison guard, Robert Mitchell, alleging sexual assault, harassment, and intimidation.

GENDERPAC, NOW MEET ON TRANSINCLUSION

[San Francisco, CA: 25 January 97] Representatives of GenderPAC and other groups make an impassioned presentation to NOW's prestigious President's Conference this afternoon, pursuing ratification of a two-year-old trans-inclusion resolution which has languished at NOW's National Board. Also in attendance at the annual roundtable held by NOW state coordinators is current NOW President, Patricia Ireland.

DEE FARMER LOSES PRISON RAPE SUIT

[Madison, WI: 26 January 97] Trans-inmate Dee Farmer, who fought all the way to the Supreme Court for her right to sue the Federal prison where she was raped, loses her suit. After deliberating only a few hours, the seven-member jury returns a verdict of not guilty, effectively closing Ms. Farmer's case. The ruling appears to give prison officials license to turn a deaf ear to gender-vulnerable inmates.

ANOTHER TRANS-MALE "RAPE" CASE

[Pacs, WA: 21 February 97] In a case ignored by the queer media, twenty-year-old transexual man Christopher Wheatley is indicted for the third-degree rape of his fifteen-year-old girlfriend. The case immediately brings to mind the charge and conviction of Colorado Springs trans-man Sean O'Neill, with charges hinging on the girlfriend's accusation that she believed Wheatley was male even after several sexual encounters. Wheatley, who has been taking hormones for two years and lives as male, is convicted and sentenced to two years in prison.

MURDER TRIAL VIGIL FOR CHANELLE PICKETT

[Cambridge, MA: 27 February 97] Thirty-five gay, lesbian, bisexual, and transgender activists gather outside the Middlesex county courthouse in a peaceful vigil for slain transexual Chanelle Pickett as the trial of William Palmer, Pickett's alleged assailant, is to begin inside. Wearing a Menace T-shirt, activist Nancy Nangeroni hands a leaflet to an obviously angry recipient, who turns out to be alleged killer William Palmer.

TRANS-PARENT DENIED CUSTODY OF CHILDREN

[St. Louis, MO: 12 March 97] Divorced transexual father Sharon Boyd, now legally female, loses joint custody of her two sons, age ten and seven, after a Missouri State Appeals court effectively rules that she constitutes an endangerment to her children. A coalition of far-right groups, including Campus Crusade for Christ and Focus on the Family, backs the mother, reportedly using this as a test case for broad political action against trans and queer parents. Three bills drawing on the decision are subsequently introduced into the Missouri state legislature.

SATURDAY NIGHT LIVE AGAIN SAVAGES TRANSPEOPLE

[New York, NY: 20 April 97] Only months after his ill-considered "joke" on the Brandon Teena murder trial verdict, *Saturday Night Live*'s Norm MacDonald comments on the Sharon Boyd custody case, "Hmmm...I wonder who's going to win this one, the mother of the two children, or the guy who had his penis twisted into a fake vagina." NBC's office of Standards and Practices is so concerned that the remarks are bleeped from the seven-second delay to the west coast. GLAAD and GenderPAC again file a joint protest with the network.

HERMAPHRODITES WITH ATTITUDE AND TRANSEXUAL MENACE PROTEST INTERSEX GENITAL MUTILATION (IGM)

[New York, NY: 2 May 97] A dozen members of Hermaphrodites With Attitude (HWA) and Transexual Menace demonstrate outside Columbia-Presbyterian Hospital, protesting its continued practice of Intersex Genital Mutilation. The demonstration draws media from *Newsweek*, ABC's *Prime Time Live*, the Canadian Broadcasting Company, and *Rolling Stone*. Declares HWA spokes-herm

Cheryl Chase, "Every major U.S. city has a hospital doing this procedure. It's time to lift the veil on the operating theater down the street from where you live."

EDDIE MURPHY PASSES "GO," GETS NATIONAL INTERVIEW, TRANS-PROSTITUTE GOES DIRECTLY TO JAIL

[Los Angeles, CA: 3 May 97] Comedian Eddie Murphy, who has often drawn fire for derogatory "jokes" aimed at women, gays, and people with AIDS, is stopped by police with a transexual working-girl in his car. While his companion is sent to jail on an outstanding warrant, Mr. Murphy goes on national television to explain that, as a Good Samaritan, he often gives rides and money to strange women at three in the morning. Asked if the check is in the mail and would he mind if his sister married one, Murphy allegedly replies, "Sure it is, and of course I wouldn't." A third question relating to oral hygiene is considered unprintable by *IYF* staffers.

ALLEGED KILLER WALKS IN PICKETT MURDER CASE

[Cambridge, MA: 16 May 97] Although a medical examiner testifies that Chanelle Pickett suffered severe head injuries and was strangled to death for at least eight minutes, a jury finds William Palmer innocent of murder and guilty on a single count of assault. Sentencing him to two years' incarceration with six months suspended, Judge Robert Barton notes, "Mr. Palmer should kiss the ground the defense counsel walks on." Observes one Menace activist at the trial, "He was rich, white, and employed; she was poor, black, a sometime sex-worker, and transgendered. If she had survived Palmer's assault, they'd probably send her to jail instead." Said Ms. Pickett's twin transgender sister, Gabrielle, "It's hell being transexual."

RESULTS OF 1ST NATIONAL SURVEY ON TRANSVIOLENCE ANNOUNCED

[New York, NY: 29 April 97] Results of 1st National Survey on Transviolence are published by GenderPAC. The survey finds that sixty percent of respondents report having been the victim of some kind of assault, including assault with a weapon, assault without a weapon, sexual assault, and rape. Ninety-five percent of the worst incidents reported involve two to three perpetrators. The study, which takes a year to distribute and compile, draws over four hundred respondents and is believed to be the only one of its kind.

CONGRESS MEMBERS SIGN ON AGAINST TRANSVIOLENCE AT LOBBYING DAY

[Washington, DC: 5 May 97] Capping two days of intense lobbying at the 2nd National Gender Lobbying Day, a dozen members of Congress sign one of three letters to Attorney General Janet Reno decrying gender-based violence. Instrumental in the successful effort is HRCF policy advocate Kris Pratt. It is believed to be the first time members of the U.S. Congress have gone on record on a trans-related issue. Signatories include Representatives Ed Towns (NY), Maurice Hinchey (NY), Ronald Dellums (CA), Caroline Maloney (NY), Mel Watt (NC), Bruce Vento (MN), William Clay (MO), Jerome Nadler (NY), Jesse Jackson, Jr. (IL), and Barney Frank (MA).

INTERSEX ACTIVISTS LOBBY U.S., CONGRESS

[Washington, DC: 6 May 97] As part of the 2nd National Gender Lobbying Day, five members of the Intersex Society of North America (ISNA) led by Executive Director Cheryl Chase conduct a groundbreaking lobbying effort on Capitol Hill to educate members of Congress about Intersex Genital Mutilation (IGM). Recent congressional legislation outlaws Female Genital Mutilation (FGM) but leaves IGM intact, although the vast majority of IGM surgeries are normal little girls with clitorises deemed "too large" by doctors, often because it is feared they will grow up to be masculinized, homosexual women.

NATIONAL NEWS DISCOVERS INTERSEX GENITAL MUTILATION (IGM)

[New York, NY: 13 May 97] A week after protests at Columbia-Presbyterian Hospital by Hermaphrodites With Attitude (HWA) and Transexual Menace and the first-ever Capitol Hill lobbying effort by the Intersex Society of North American (ISNA), major news stories about IGM appear in the *New York Times* and *Newsweek*. *Dateline NBC* begins preparing a much-anticipated segment for airing June 16, while ABC's *Prime Time Live* starts interviewing ISNA members for a piece to be broadcast in the fall.

HRCF Prepares to Re-Introduce ENDA, Gender Protection Still Missing

[Washington, DC: 10 May 97] Elation among gender activists over advances on Capitol Hill is tempered by reports that HRCF is set to re-introduce the Employment Non-Discrimination Bill (ENDA) on June 23. The omission of gender expression from ENDA wording still leaves millions of gay, lesbian, bisexual, and transgender Americans vulnerable to being fired for not looking or acting sufficiently straight.

Landmark Meeting with Department of Justice on Gender-Based Violence

[Washington, DC: 13 May 97] In a landmark meeting, GenderPAC, NGLTF, HRCF, and BiNet USA meet with Assistant Attorney General Eleanor Dean Acheson and members of DOJ's Office of Policy Development to present letters on transviolence from U.S. Congress members and discuss hate crimes against differently gendered Americans. The meeting is requested by GenderPAC after the bombing of Atlanta's "Otherside" is covered as a gay and lesbian hate crime although the bar is well-known for its bisexual and transgender clientele. Letters addressed to Attorney General Reno decrying gender-based violence are presented from eleven members of Congress. Declares Alex Beckles of Rep. Ed Towns' (NY) office, the first U.S. Representative to sign a statement on transgender people, "Ed Towns feels strongly that no American—be they gay or straight, black or white, or transgendered—should be the target of violence or have to live with the fear of violence."

GENDERPAC ADDRESSES NOW NATIONAL BOARD ON TRANS-INCLUSION

[Memphis, TN: 3 July 97] Through the efforts of NOW President Patricia Ireland, National Lesbian Rights Coordinator Kimberlee Ward, and New Jersey State President Bear Atwood, representatives of GenderPAC are invited to address the National Board at the annual National Conference. In a taut half-hour session which draws close questioning, presenters suggest it is time feminists stop policing who can call themselves a woman and get on with the business of pursuing feminist goals. They close with a plea for support for the cause of hundreds of intersexed girls who are genitally cut in U.S. hospitals every year.

MEMBER OF NYC S/M COMMUNITY FOUND MURDERED

[New York, NY: 2 July 97] Nadia Frey, who sometimes worked as a dominant under the name "Mistress Hilda," is found murdered in her apartment. As with gay and transgender murders, media and police immediately speculate that her "bizarre" and "deviant" lifestyle caused the crime, effectively blaming her for her own murder. In an antidefamation letter sent to all parties, the National Coalition for Sexual Freedom (NCSF) declares, "Holding those involved in alternative sexual and affectional practice up for ridicule only feeds the perception that we are disposable people. It makes it more likely that such murders will reoccur, and less likely that they will be vigorously prosecuted."

NEW GROUP ON CAPITOL HILL

[Washington, DC: 5 July 97] Representatives of the National Coalition for Sexual Freedom (NCSF) make the rounds on Capitol Hill today, meeting informally with a number of Congressmembers and progressive organizations. States NCSF Executive Director Susan Wright, "The bottom line is—we are people who lose our jobs, our children, and sometimes our lives because of sexual or affectional preference. All we are seeking is equal rights." She announces the launching of a National Survey on Sexual and Affectional Violence.

NOW Passes Trans-Inclusion Resolution

[Memphis, TN: 6 July 97] On the final day of its National Conference, NOW passes a trans-inclusion resolution. The vote comes after extensive floor discussion and debate on seven different amendments. "This was a landmark vote. [It's an] acknowledgment that the transgender community is today's cutting edge [in] the pioneering work of exposing artificial gender constructs and breaking down the stereotypes and barriers which divide us," declares NOW Action Vice-President, Rosemary Dempsey. Agrees GenderPAC's Terri McCorkell, "In its own way, this was as historic a moment as NOW's affirmation of lesbian inclusion over twenty-five years ago....It was a truly emotional moment seeing nearly every hand in the Convention go up in support. Women who had worked on this for three years were crying and hugging in the aisles."

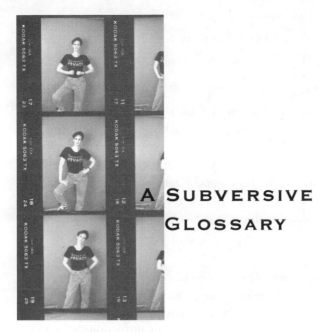

A Subversive Glossary

APIT (AY-PIT).

Acronym for A Politically Incorrect Term. Not to be confused with *aped*, meaning "to imitate or mimic." Note that *aped* itself is considered APIT if you are in the company of nonhuman higher primates (for instance monkeys, chimps, or gorillas), or if you are a nonhuman higher primate.

BISEXUAL.

The ability, in fact the desire, to have sex with anyone at anytime: as Bi-Net USA's national magazine puts it, "Anything That Moves." I'm sorry, that was all horribly APIT. Bisexuality: an erotic, romantic and/or affectional attraction for persons of either gender (assuming, of course, that there are only two).

BIOLOGICAL WOMAN.

Terribly APIT expression used by transexual women with advanced cases of NTE (see *Nontransexual Envy*), and nontransexual women trying to distinguish themselves from trannies.

BUTLER, JUDITH.

An American feminist theorist and philosopher. Her book *GenderTrouble* marks the most far-reaching and penetrating critique of feminism, sexuality, and binary sex from a postmodern viewpoint to date. Unfortunately, as with the work of Michel Foucault, we are still waiting for a good English-language translation.

CLOCKED (VERB).

See *Read.*

DISCOURSE.

In everyday usage, it simply means conversation. Foucault and many others used it more to refer to authoritative speech: those voices within a common speech community who are listened to, whose utterances are commonly accepted as true by other members. These include the voices from academia, the legal system, the medical establishment, and so on.

ERASURE, OPPOSITIONAL, MARGINALIZE.

Political processes carried out in discourse. *Oppositional* refers to the construction of binaries in which one thing is made to stand against, in polar contrast to, another, e.g., masculine and feminine. *Marginalize* refers to discounting the worth or weight of someone or some group, politically or within cultural discourse. *Erasure* refers to keeping something off the cultural map of language to begin with, so that it hasn't even attained the status of marginalization. This includes genders that we haven't yet named, or genitals not allowed to exist or relegated to the status of disease.

ESSENTIALIZE.

Close to *naturalize;* to assume a feature is an essential property of something, as in sex is an essential property of bodies.

F-TO-M, "FEMALE TO MALE."

An APIT way to describe anyone, as if we were trolley cars in transit from one sex to another; a transexual man.

FOUCAULT, MICHEL.

An influential French philosopher everyone quotes, no one has read, and everyone enjoys disagreeing with.

GENDERBASHING.

The harassment, abuse, or assault of genderqueers based on gender norms.

GENDER DYSPHORIA.

A discomfort with one's gender; a term used by nontransexual shrinks who write surgery letters. Not used very often outside medical and psychiatric circles because most people either don't know what *dysphoria* means, or think it's a medicinal compound like Fletchers Castoria, which you take for the trots.

GENDER IDENTITY CONFLICT (APIT).

I don't know...does your gender feel in conflict? Mine doesn't. Like *Gender Dysphoria*, above, "a discomfort with one's gender; a term used by nontransexual shrinks who write surgery letters." Also used extensively by people who are uncomfortable saying *transexual.*

GenderPAC, GENDER PUBLIC ADVOCACY COALITION.

A national not-for-profit group, composed of individuals and organizations dedicated to pursuing "gender, affectional, and racial equality" and contesting gender-based oppression.

GENDERPHOBIA.

A fear and hatred of different genders.

GENDERPATHOPHILIA.

(1) An obsessive fear or need to pathologize any kind of gender behavior that makes you feel uncomfortable; (2) a dread disease that strikes nine out of ten American psychiatrists.

"THE GENDER CHALLENGED."

Just don't start with me, okay?

GENETIC WOMAN.

See *Biological Woman.*

HERMAPHRODITES WITH ATTITUDE (HWA).

A direct action/protest group for intersexuals.

HERMOPHOBIC.

An unnatural fear of or discomfort toward intersexuals and hermaphrodites.

INSCRIBE.

Addresses the concept that the meanings we attach to bodies are not just "found" there, but written or *inscribed* there by us.

INTERSEX GENITAL MUTILATION (IGM).

The homegrown version of Female Genital Mutilation. The Intersex Society of North America estimates that about five intersexed children have their genitals cut into in U.S. hospitals every day for cosmetic reasons, a procedure performed by accredited surgeons and covered by all major insurance plans.

INTERSEXUALITY.

(1) A psychiatric emergency on the part of doctors and parents that is treated by operating on the genitals of the infant; (2) a condition in which someone is born with technicolor genitals while everyone else's are black and white.

"JUST A CROSSDRESSER."

A phrase employed by some transexuals to indicate that if you change your body you are somehow "more serious" than someone who just puts on a dress.

M-TO-F, "MALE TO FEMALE."

See *F-to-M.* APIT expression to describe a transexual woman.

M-TO-F-TO-M, "MALE TO FEMALE TO MALE."

What I am when addressed as *Sir*, which is about half the time.

Magic Wand.

The thing that, if you're a tranny and still have it, they make you use the Maintenance Restroom in the basement. Not to be confused with the famous Hitachi Magic Wand.

Marginalize.

See *Erasure*.

Naturalize.

Issuing directly from Nature, and thus unmediated by language, context, past, or you and me. See *Essentialize*.

Nontransexual.

A person who is not transexual. (The term is descriptive only and not pejorative.)

Nontransexual Envy (NTE).

A particularly dismal and unnecessary psychological affliction which strikes transexual people in their prime, often those who present perfectly well as normal, healthy transexual men and women. NTE is characterized chiefly by shame, self-hate, and extreme closet-bound behavior.

Oppositional.

See *Erasure*.

Passing.

The act of trying to convince nontransexuals that one is also nontransexual. (The word isn't exactly APIT, but the action, the very *idea!*)

Political.

Not in the usual sense, as in Democrats or Republicans, nor even in the liberal tradition to refer to the Power of the State. The power that circulates between members of a community in every small interaction based on common practices and beliefs (e.g., *discourse*).

POSTMODERN.

Oh God. Trying to write a brief definition of *postmodernism* is like begging two hundred academics to apply tit-clamps (not that that would necessarily be a bad thing, but...). A movement spawned by French philosopher Jacques Derrida, among others, that proclaimed the end of modern Enlightenment notions of authenticity, truth, and reason as a single grand, eternal narrative by which all things could be fairly judged. Part of its thrust was to open up repressive and monolithic notions of truth to those realities and experiences which are nonrational, small, and local—even to those which cannot be put into the confines of words. Derrida did this by looking at the hidden, underlying assumptions that allowed various truths to operate as capital *T* Truth (also known as deconstruction). Foucault took a different tack, focusing on the political effects—who gained or lost power—when notions of sexuality became "natural truths" instead of cultural products. Many academics are busy debunking postmodernism, i.e., explaining why it is dead, pointless, or (for the truly creative) both dead *and* pointless. Such angst roughly translates to the uncomfortable awareness that postmodernism undermines precisely those sorts of authoritative claims to Objective Knowledge that enable academics to get paid for pronouncing it. (Okay, bring on the clamps.)

PSYCHIATRIC ABUSE OF GENDER-VARIANT CHILDREN (PAGC).

The use of psychiatric diagnosis of Gender Identity Disorder to pathologize and enforce treatment on gender-variant or so-called pre-homosexual children, including psychotherapy, behavior modification, or confinement on locked psychiatric wards. Documented in Phyllis Burke's book, *Gender Shock,* as well as in an autobiography by PAGC survivor Daphne Scholinski, *The Last Time I Wore A Dress.*

READ (VERB).

Correctly identified as a transexual, as in, "I was immediately read by this snotty little thirteen-year-old on the street yesterday—you know, young girls can clock you at two hundred paces on a moonless night."

REAL.

What *any* gender is until the exact moment you become aware that you're performing it—then it becomes *drag*.

REAL LIFE TEST (RLT).

No, this is not a joke. This is what doctors call it when you find out if nontransexual bigots are going to kill you when you try to live in your preferred gender role. If you lose your job due to gender discrimination, you flunk your RLT. Or you may pass, but you can no longer afford surgery, so it's irrelevant.

REAL WOMAN.

See *Biological Woman*. See *Genetic Woman*.

SEMIOTICS.

The science or theory of signs.

SIGNS.

Anything that means something to somebody: words, pictures, gestures, sounds, etc.

SOMATIC DYSPHORIA.

A discomfort with one's body; the correct form for the misnamed *Gender Dysphoria*.

SPOKESHERM.

An intersexual after she has seen the urologist, had surgery, grown up, and realized what was done to her. See *Hermaphrodites With Attitude*.

SRS.

Sex Reassignment Surgery, i.e., sex-change surgery.

STANDARDS OF CARE.

Something invented by professionals to protect us widdle transpeople from hurting our widdle selves with sharp things. A series of guidelines propagated by doctors and health professionals for deciding who gets to have hormones and surgery. See *God, Playing At*.

T-BIRD.

Someone who likes, admires, or is attracted to transexuals. Can be dismissive or affectionate, depending upon the speaker.

TITWB (TIT-WIB).

Acronym for Trapped In The Wrong Body (APIT); a phrase used mainly by transexuals in television soap operas, transexuals trying to convince skeptical surgeons that they should sharpen up the old scalpel, or transexuals trying to break the bad news to hysterical family members who suddenly flash on the nightmare feeling of being stuck in a television soap opera. No one is trapped in the wrong body, although many of us are trapped in the wrong culture.

TRANFAN.

See *T-Bird.*

TRANSMEN.

(1) Transexual men; (2) an extremely handsome group of people who are going to be very upset with me for not saying enough about them in this book; (3) people I am going to have to suck up to a lot to get back in their good graces.

TRANSPHOBIA.

A fear and hatred of changing sexual characteristics. As my friend Lynn Walker puts it, "Discrimination based on the shape of one's skin."

TRANSITION.

The process of moving from one socially recognized gender to the other. (Naturally there are only two choices here.) This involves presenting oneself as "culturally appropriate." With transexual women, this customarily means donning the traditional female rig: dresses, high heels, and make-up. Only in this culture could the throwing off of decades of gender oppression, dating from infancy, be called *transition.*

Tribify (TRI-beh-fi).

To naturalize one's own gender, genitals, or sex by successfully constructing those of the subject under investigation (i.e., transpeople and other genderqueers) as products of some quaint practice by a bizarre and exotic tribe.

Ubiquitous (you-BIK-qwi-tuss).

Present, or seeming to be present, everywhere at the same time; as in "by the Middle Ages, Greek philosophy, art and culture were ubiquitous among Pan-Hellenic cultures." Nothing at all to do with transexuality, but a damn fine word to know and use. Also, my tenth-grade English teacher, Helen Davis, told us to remember it and use it often. Bet you never thought it'd show up in a book on transexuality, did you, Helen?

Weekend Warrior.

Transpeople who dress up and go out only on weekends; akin to "transpires," transpeople who only come out at night.

Woman-Born-Woman.

See *Biological Woman*. See *Genetic Woman*. See *Real Woman*. See a shrink.

Women-Born-Women Only.

Perhaps the definitive APIT phrase; derived from the concept that women are born, not made, just like track stars, tormented Irish poets, and gifted chefs. *Women-Born-Women Only* appears mainly on the bottom of flyers for lesbian events, promoted by those who want to discriminate against transexuals, without alerting other attendees that we're being kept out. Like a secret signal or a Masonic handshake.

Woodwork (verb).

Woodworking; to go back into the woodwork; refers to transexuals who attempt to blend in or pass.

Firebrand Books is an award-winning feminist and lesbian pub-
lishing house. We are committed to producing quality work in a
wide variety of genres by ethnically and racially diverse authors.
Now in our twelfth year, we have over ninety titles in print.

A free catalog is available on request from Firebrand Books, 141
The Commons, Ithaca, New York 14850, (607) 272-0000.